A Cup of Comfort

for Mothers & Sons

Stories that celebrate a
very special bond

Edited by
Colleen Sell

ADAMS MEDIA
Avon, Massachusetts

For my son, Mickey, and for the moms and sons dearest to my heart:
Jennifer and Scotty; Christie and brand-new baby John; Jeannie,
Scott, Daniel, and Patrick; Melinda, Arren, and Matt; Jeanne and Nikk

Copyright ©2005, F+W Publications, Inc.
All rights reserved. This book, or parts thereof, may not be reproduced
in any form without permission from the publisher; exceptions
are made for brief excerpts used in published reviews.

A Cup of Comfort is a trademark of F+W Publications, Inc.

Published by
Adams Media, an F+W Publications Company
57 Littlefield Street, Avon, MA 02322. U.S.A.
www.adamsmedia.com and *www.cupofcomfort.com*

ISBN: 1-59337-257-4

Printed in Canada.

J I H G F E D C B A

Library of Congress Cataloging-in-Publication Data
A cup of comfort for mothers and sons / edited by Colleen Sell.
p.   cm.
ISBN 1-59337-257-4
1. Mothers and sons. 2. Conduct of life. I. Sell, Colleen.
HQ755.85.C8563 2005
306.874'3—dc22

2004026391

This publication is designed to provide accurate and authoritative information
with regard to the subject matter covered. It is sold with the understanding that
the publisher is not engaged in rendering legal, accounting, or other professional
advice. If legal advice or other expert assistance is required, the services of a
competent professional person should be sought.
—From a *Declaration of Principles* jointly adopted by a Committee of the
American Bar Association and a Committee of Publishers and Associations

Many of the designations used by manufacturers and sellers to distinguish
their products are claimed as trademarks. Where those designations appear in
this book and Adams Media was aware of a trademark claim, the designations
have been printed with initial capital letters.

This book is available at quantity discounts for bulk purchases.
For information, please call 1-800-872-5627.

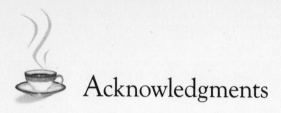

Acknowledgments

My gratitude and admiration go to the mothers and sons whose honest and beautiful stories grace these pages.

My deep appreciation goes to the kind and talented team at Adams Media. Special thanks go to Kate Epstein, Kirsten Amann, Laura MacLaughlin, Kate McBride, Gene Molter, Beth Gissinger, and Gary Krebs for their support and contributions to the *Cup of Comfort* book series.

I am most grateful to Paula Munier, my colleague and friend of twenty years, for creating the *Cup of Comfort* series and for reaching out to me in my darkest hour, when my mother's heart was breaking for her broken son, and convincing me and the powers that be that I was the right editor for the job.

Thanks to my son and to my mother and my brothers, my sister and my nephews, my daughters and my grandsons, my mother-in-law and my husband for showing me just how sweet it is, this mother-son connection.

Contents

Introduction

Sons are for fathers. So goes the party line. And I believed it . . . until I gazed into the sweet, old-soul face of my newborn son and knew the real truth: Sons are for mothers, too.

Still, during my son's growing-up years, I found it difficult to completely ignore the advice of "experts" and well-meaning loved ones who discouraged close relationships between mothers and sons. Some said it was unwise, potentially even harmful, for a son to form a close bond with his mother. Others claimed it was simply not possible, that the natural order of things is for boys to distance themselves from their mothers. As the young and conscientious mom of a first (and only) son, I often found myself weighing my strong instinct to nurture our mother-son relationship against the fear that getting too close might somehow thwart or damage his "maleness."

What utter nonsense, I realize now. Thankfully, my instincts won out most of the time. And from the day my bouncing baby boy made his grand entrance twenty-eight years ago, the two of us have shared a bond that is as deep, strong, abiding, rich, and natural as any mother-daughter and any father-son connection could be. But it *is* different, in some ways.

While growing up, my son was always a bit of a mystery to me. Unlike his two older sisters—whose emotions, thought processes, and behavior I could usually anticipate and understand—my son as often as not baffled me. He would say or do something, and I'd think, *Huh? What is that about? Where did that come from?* When I did unravel the whys and wherefores behind his alien behavior—when I figured out (more or less) what he was thinking and feeling—I was even more surprised. His perspective was definitely different from mine.

Frankly, I rather enjoyed the element of surprise and the journey of discovery that having a close relationship with my son allowed. As confusing and frustrating as the mismatch of our wavelengths could be, it was also intriguing and enlightening, often endearing, and sometimes flat-out funny. In discovering what made my "tiny man" tick, I learned a lot about the male psyche and about myself, as both a mother and a woman.

Our open and honest relationship also enabled me to provide my son with some insight into—and, I hope, a deeper appreciation for—the female perspective. I was determined to help him become a manly man who was also a gentleman. Sometimes, I might have gone a little overboard in my mission.

One of the meanest things I ever said to my son was in response to his complaint, when asked to do dishes, about having to do "girls' work." It was the third time he'd griped about being assigned "girly" household chores. The first two times, I'd explained that the only fair and valid qualification for determining someone's right or responsibility to do a task was ability. He could do dishes as well as I could take out trash. I'd explained that being relegated to a job you didn't want to do and being prohibited from doing a job you wanted to do simply because of your gender was demeaning. This was a hot button for me, and he knew it. So, on his third gripe, I snapped. In anger, I called him a "sexist little pig" and assigned him dinner dishes for the entire week.

That night, shortly after I'd gone to bed, I heard sobs coming from my son's bedroom. He was fourteen; crying wasn't cool, and he rarely did it. I went to his room, sat on his bed, and stroking his spiky hair, I asked him what was wrong.

"You hate me," he said, his voice cracking on "hate."

"Sweetheart, I do not hate you. I love you with all my heart," I said.

"How can you love me if you think I'm a sexist pig? You hate sexist pigs!" he wailed.

I apologized for calling him a nasty name and hurting his feelings. But, I explained once again, it was important to me that he understand that sexism, like racism and other forms of prejudice, is offensive and hurtful, too.

"I understand, Mom," he said. "I'm sorry."

"I'm sorry, too," I said. "Truce?"

"Truce."

We shook pinky fingers, and then I kissed his forehead and I stood to head back to bed.

"Mom?"

"Yes?"

"Do I still have to do dishes every night this week?"

"Yes."

Silence, followed by a deep sigh.

"Love you, Mom."

"Love you, Son."

That's how it is with my son and me. No matter how far apart our points of view might be, no matter how upset we might get with one another, it always comes down to that: a truce. An eternal alliance. A loving, respectful acceptance of our differences. A joyful celebration of our commonalities. An unbreakable, unshakable bond.

There was a time, though, when I thought we'd

lost our connection—and, worse, that I'd lost my son, and worst, that he'd lost himself, to a debilitating brain injury and resultant neurobiological disorder. During the first five years following the brain injury, my son was disconnected from reality, and from me, much of the time. Though I barely recognized him and though he repeatedly pushed me away, I tried unceasingly to reach and reconnect with the beautiful boy whose gentle soul I'd known even before his birth. As he sat or paced in stonewalled silence, distant and distracted, I would quietly recount, over and over again, every special moment, every magical connection, we had shared as a family and as mother and son.

I reminded him of our nightly ritual, which began when he was a toddler and extended all the way through high school. Just before drifting off to sleep, he would call out from his room, "Love you, Mama/ Mommy/Mom," and I would answer, "Love you, Son." Even when he slept over at his dad's or someone else's house, he couldn't sleep until we'd exchanged our "love you" routine over the phone.

I recalled how, when I was carrying him in my tummy, he'd "dance" when I played my favorite tunes— Joni Mitchell, the Beatles, Paul Simon, Motown. How, before he could walk, he'd grab my fingers with his dimpled hands, pull himself up, and shake his dia-pered booty to the grooves. How, as a teen—when his buddies weren't around—he'd play his guitar along to my old tapes. How we'd sing out loud together in the car, sometimes making up outrageously silly songs, like a country-western parody that began with the line, "My wife done left me for the butcher in the holler."

I recalled how, when he was a baby, I'd hum while I rocked him and coo, "*Ahhh*, my tiny man." One evening, when he was no more than two or three months old, as I rocked and hummed and cooed to him, I was startled by a strange sound, almost like a frog croaking, and realized it was my little one "*ahhhing*" right along with me.

I retold the story of our drive home from preschool one afternoon, when he enthusiastically obeyed my request to refasten his seatbelt.

"Thank you," I said. "You are such a good little boy."

"No, my not!" he said.

"You're *not* a good little boy?" I asked.

"I'm not a little boy."

"Oh, excuse me . . . you're right. You're a very good *big* boy."

"No . . . ," he said, exasperated. "I'm a tiny man."

My tiny man, I wanted to add, but didn't then nor all those years later when I was trying to remind him of who he was, who I was, who we were. Instead, I reminded him of the many times when he'd been, indeed, my tiny man—my most ardent admirer and most mighty protector. I told him about the time we were at a baseball game and a fellow spectator paid a little too much attention to yours truly. My son stood up on the seat next to me, stretched on tiptoes to his full three-feet height, puffed out his Superman T-shirted chest, wrapped his meaty little arm around my neck in a death grip, fixed his evil eye on my admirer, and between clenched teeth growled, "She's *my* mama!"

In recalling these and countless other precious mother-son memories, I was saying to my lost boy, *I am your mama! I will always be your mama. Our bond shall not be broken. I will not let go of you or give up on you. I will hold on to you and keep on reaching for you until you find your way back.*

And he did, thanks in large part to an exceptional doctor, to medical science, and to my son's own courage and tenacity. But I also know, without a shadow of a doubt, that our close relationship helped pull him, and me, through the darkness and back into the light. It gave us hope and understanding, comfort and strength. Today, our bond is deeper than ever, our relationship closer than ever. And I look forward to discovering new mysteries and joys as the mother of a son who has grown up to be an exceptional human being . . . and quite the manly gentleman.

In *A Cup of Comfort for Mothers & Sons*, you will discover many tender and telling stories about real-life mothers and sons. Some of the stories will tug at your heartstrings; others will tickle your funny bone. As a collection, these stories reveal the depth and breadth, and capture the magic and beauty, of the special bond between mothers and sons. And each story provides living testimony to something those of us blessed with close mother-son relationships already know: Sons are for mothers, too.

Enjoy!

Colleen Sell

Ice Cubes

I heard ice cubes rattling and turned to see my adult son pouring a Coke. Talking a blue streak, he grabbed the last ice from the bin and emptied out four new trays. Tall, broad-shouldered, and handsome, he looked every inch a man. But I needed one last bit of proof that he was well launched into adulthood, so I watched.

He filled the trays with water and replaced them in the freezer. I gave him ten points, rejoicing at how far we've both come. During his adolescence, ice cubes had triggered our biggest fight.

Just old enough to have his own set of car keys jingling in his pocket, he had developed an ice cube passion. My husband and I went to sleep at night to crunching sounds coming from his bedroom and were frequently jarred awake an hour later as he mindlessly rattled more cubes in a plastic mug. Ice cubes were his crutch, his pacifier.

Though I worried about possible damage to his teeth, that he didn't refill the empty trays rankled me even more. Our neighbors grew accustomed to my appearance at 5:30 P.M., clutching an ice bucket like a saffron-clad Tibetan monk with a begging bowl.

In increasingly heated exchanges, I stressed that it wasn't about ice as much as it was about responsibility within the family. Ice cubes became the metaphor for all of my issues with his teenaged self-centeredness. As the empty trays remained unfilled, my complaints veered off into his messy bedroom, dirty dishes left on the kitchen counter, smeared toothpaste on the bathroom sink, or his car parked across our driveway. The list went on and on, but it always began and ended with ice cubes.

One evening at dinnertime, after a difficult day at work, I opened the freezer for ice. Nothing. Furious, I turned and saw the empty trays at the far end of the counter. Gripping one tray like a war club, I rounded on my son and, if words could do bodily harm, he might still be in a cast. As it was, I yelled, he swore, I hit him on the arm with the empty tray, he pushed me against the counter, and I screamed, "Out!"

In tears of rage, he slammed out the door, and I threw the tray against the wall.

I stood still, ashamed of the things I had said but certain that all fault lay with my son. My husband shook his head sorrowfully and made another trip next door with the ice bucket. My son circled the house, came in the front door, and went upstairs to his room. As the rest of us ate dinner, his unoccupied chair spoke volumes.

At bedtime, I listened outside his door. Silence. I knocked, and when he didn't throw something at the door, I interpreted it as permission to enter.

He lay with one arm across his eyes. His adolescent body filled the narrow bed, and my memory flew back in time to when he was nine months old. I heard once again his palms slapping against the wooden floors as he crawled at top speed toward me when I came home from work. Chubby hands then, with grubby bits of graham cracker stuck between the fingers. Now those same hands were broad and tanned, with tendons where lovely dimples once lurked. Scrapes from dirt bike injuries marred his knuckles. His broken nails needed trimming, but I no longer had the job of imprisoning his fat little hands to clip the fingernails after his nightly bath.

His overlapping bare feet looked like Christ's on the cross, pale and long and narrow. A surfing sock line separated his chalky feet from the deep tan above. Peeking from beneath his frayed cutoffs were knobby knees scarred by surfboard collisions with coral reefs. Those same knees had been his most ticklish spot in infancy, and I ached to once again squeeze the flesh above them. I wanted others to love him as much as

I did. I wanted a guarantee that his selfish, thought-less behavior would disappear and that he would turn into the mature, compassionate son I had always expected to raise.

What had I done wrong?

I knew I couldn't touch him, not yet, but in my heart I yearned to kiss his fingertips or bury my nose in the sweaty male scent of his tousled hair. I wanted to whisper my love, to hold him in my arms and sing "Kumbaya" once more.

Instead, I knelt and said, "Colin, I'm so sorry I lost my temper, but I don't know what to do. When you don't refill the ice cube trays, it drives me crazy."

Only a strangled sniff came from the bed.

I touched him. He didn't flinch, so I held his hand. He squeezed my fingers, and my heart soared like a bird released from a cage.

"Mom . . . ," he began, but paused.

I kissed his fingers and waited for him to collect himself.

He tried again. "Mom, there's something I don't understand. I just don't understand why you get so upset about this."

I took a deep breath, choking back a resurgence of irritation. *Speak calmly*, I told myself. "Because when you leave us without any ice cubes, it makes me . . ."

He lowered his arm with a jerk and stared up at the ceiling. "Mom, listen to me. Just *listen*, will you?

Look. I've never been arrested. I don't use drugs. I don't smoke. I've never gotten a DUI. I always let you know where I am. And I've never gotten a girl pregnant."

He paused, turned his head, and stared at me. His chin trembled as he continued, "I just don't understand why you get so upset about *ice cubes*!"

Ice cubes.

I swallowed around an enormous lump in my throat. Then I kissed his damp forehead. Looking into those blue, blue eyes, I relaxed for the first time in hours.

"I'll make a deal with you," I said. "You keep taking care of all that stuff, and from now on I'll take care of the ice cubes."

Every afternoon until he left for college, I emptied ice cubes into the bin and refilled the trays. First thing each morning I did it again. I made so much ice every day that he never had to deal with the trays at all. I kept my part of the bargain, and he kept his.

I figured that, by far, I got the better part of the deal.

Peggy Vincent

This story was first published as "Tensions at Home Suddenly Thaw" in the *Christian Science Monitor*, September 15, 2000.

# Hero

My hero never carried me out of a burning building or cracked a walnut with his biceps. He did not earn a Purple Heart or a boxing championship. He is no famous quarterback, and he does not have the leading-man looks of Robert Redford. He is no Aeneas, Spartacus, or Hamlet—a legend beyond his time. My hero has not even come of age yet, for he is my six-year-old son, William.

I had the first glimpse of my son's unique brand of quiet heroism when his sister was born and screamed her head off the first three months of her life. William exhibited no sibling rivalry or jealousy, but instead showed sympathy for my inability to console colicky Caroline. He did not ask me why I was running the vacuum cleaner again just so I would not hear her rage in the other room. He understood without being told how frustrated I was when I got up repeatedly to go to her room. One time, he told me to sit down, that he would take care of it. And he did. I can still see him walking into her room, his little redhead barely tall enough to peep inside the high crib. With his arm at an odd angle, he patted her tense back with his chubby little hand, cooing, "Hush, little sister. Don't cry." Hearing her brother's voice, she grew quiet momentarily.

I can still feel his hand on my back, too, when I—crazed with postpartum blues—was sobbing because Caroline would not stop crying. I saw the concern in his eyes, and I witnessed his exemplary big-man behavior. He was my rock in a house full of wailing women. He saved my life right then and there—and he might have even saved the life of his infant sister. He was three years old.

Though mother-son relationships are often special, my bond with William was extraordinary for the telepathy we shared. For example, for a while, I felt a certain irritation with complete strangers who would walk up to my one-year-old daughter, stoop down to the stroller, and pinch her in the cheek or kiss her on the head. One day, I found myself in an elevator with Caroline in the stroller and William standing next to me. In walked an elderly lady with blue hair and arthritic hands. The moment she saw Caroline's dimpled cheeks, she reached out her clawlike hand. *Here we go again*, I thought. At that moment, William hissed with the venom of a snake,

"Stop! Don't you touch her!" The lady's outstretched arm froze in midair.

A more heroic example of our connectedness occurred when William's three-year-old girlfriend was so enamored with the falling snow that she started running to catch the flakes, not noticing the busy street she was heading toward. Just as I was thinking of racing after her, William hollered and dashed after his friend, then overtook her and threw his toddler body in front of her—much to her mother's gratitude. This was truly one of his more heroic acts in the conventional sense, but William's heroism has often been most sublime when he has exhibited insight and empathy beyond his years.

I mean, I knew I had an unusual child when William, at three, told me he had "terrible heartburn again." At first I ascribed the comment to his having watched too many Maalox commercials, but then, when he told me, at four, he was missing his "other, normal life," I began to seriously wonder.

"What do you mean by that?" I asked, sitting down next to him.

William rolled his eyes to underscore his feeling that mothers exist to ask inane questions, and then he replied, "Because . . . I really miss my wife and kids." His voice broke, but like kids are wont to do, he moved on immediately. He jumped off the couch, raced into the front yard, and hopped onto his tricycle like a hardened cowboy.

"Well, he could have been referring to a previous life," crackled my sister over the long-distance phone line. Although I didn't want to rule out anything, because death and otherworldly matters give me the creeps, I was skeptical. So, I wrote it off as the kind of "old soul" remark William was able to make simply because his powers of observation, imagination, and articulation were more advanced than those of most kids his age.

However, when his little preschool friend, Elise, came over for lunch one day, I had another insight into William's connection with "The Beyond." While riding in our car, Elise and William exchanged views about God and church. As the driver, I relish such moments, because young kids are remarkably candid in the backseat of a car, probably because they think nobody's listening, giving me all the more reason to eavesdrop. The topic of Heaven came up, and Elise giggled like an older schoolgirl, eyebrows raised and laughter coming out in snorts and hiccups. William did not share her hilarity. On the contrary, he pulled his train engineer cap farther down his face and stared solemnly out of the window.

Then he said, "Well, I can remember Heaven rather clearly. I even think I remember God."

Elise thought this was hysterical and bounced up and down in her car seat with glee.

Clenching his jaw, William continued as if in a trancelike state. "There were goats. It was good. I liked it."

After these revelations, there followed a brief cooling-off period between William and Elise. When I later asked him whether they were still friends, he sighed with the sophistication of someone who has had years of therapy and said, "Mom, Elise and I have a very complicated relationship."

To me, William's heroism lies in these kinds of comments. It seems he has had a whole life behind him already—a life in which he has faced, and learned from, moral dilemmas. He never was a child; he was always a little man. He even dressed like one: pants with cuffs, dress shirts, ties, penny loafers. People would ask me whether we had come from a funeral, because William was always so dressed up. One blazing hot summer he refused to wear shorts because they were not "fashionable" enough. (I think he meant "formal.") I remember him sitting in the sandbox at the park, his cheeks flaming red, his tie getting in the way as he scooped up sand.

Now, at almost-seven, he will not come near a button-down shirt, or tie, or penny loafers. But his old-soul style has remained, and with it comes a compassion that has made him a hero among his peers too. William stands up for the weaker ones in his class. He was outraged the other day when one of the boys characterized a shy girl as someone "you can push aside" because she "has no feelings to begin with." In the playground, William protects his little sister like a lion, a role she has gratefully acknowledged by calling him "Daddy" when her real daddy is out of town.

In a culture that is fed by adventure movies, crashing cars, and blazing guns, the conventional hero is often male, good-looking, and muscular: Rambo. But as a woman, I am much more drawn to the anti-Rambo, the kind of sensitive guy who can talk about his feelings without losing his backbone—the kind of man who does not have to put on any bravado. William is such a guy, and as his mother, I cherish his sensitive qualities as grand and gutsy assets that will serve him better than countless hours of pumping weights in the gym.

William and I don't have telepathic moments anymore, and our early intimacy has now given way to play dates, school, and sports. I see my role in his life receding into the background, and I am trying to be brave about it. Recently, I made my first long-distance trip away from him (and his father and sister). I tried not to think too much of it when he told me on the phone, with the indifference of a teenager, that he didn't really miss me. That is when I realized I had lost my sensitive and precocious little William, who, on a second call, did not even bother to come to the phone. On the third day, when I called again, I secretly rejoiced when his father told me William had peed in his bed, an accident that has never happened in my presence. I tried not to overanalyze, telling myself that bedwetting didn't necessarily mean he was missing me or experiencing some maternal separation anxiety.

When I saw his happy face at the airport, I thought, *Yes, he did miss me. Or does he just know about the presents in my suitcase?* But I knew for certain that our connection was intact when, at home, he wanted to cuddle, his long legs dangling off my "shrunken" lap, and when, just before he drifted off to sleep, he told me he was worried that Julia Child would no longer cook now that she had turned ninety.

"And Mom, did you know that a killer whale is not a whale but a dolphin?"

I told him I did not, and felt tempted to ask him if he knew he'd had a wife and kids in a former life. But I refrained, because . . . well, even heroes need to grow up and even old souls need to be children.

Inez Hollander

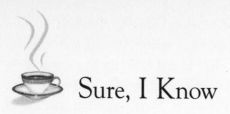 # Sure, I Know

Tom rocked slowly, rhythmically, his head bobbing in time. The chair by the living room window had been his refuge and haven, his vantage point set at a safe distance from the passing world outside. It was a gentle rocking that afforded him a virtual hypnotic escape into a detachment safe from the bustling masses, which he did not understand and that had no time for his simple ways. He had kept his vigil for all these many years, softly murmuring to himself remembrances of yesterdays. He watched. He listened. Mostly he rocked.

Today, turning toward the kitchen, he gazed at his sister, Nina, who now moved about intent on arranging a lunch tray for Mama. He took comfort in the thought that Nina had always appeared from somewhere whenever there was a need, like the day Papa died and she had come to take care of things.

A deep frown creased Tom's brow, as he recalled that morning when they took his father away. Mama had pulled him aside to tell him that Papa was gone, but then she was enveloped by all the people who had come to pay respects. Nina had been there, and it relieved him to catch her looking at him from time to time. Tom had rocked and stared, but felt unable to slip away into his realm of whispered memories, for grief was new to him and made him wonder about the world even more than before. When night did come, the house turned cold and empty. He had never turned in until Papa gave the word, which Tom, in his dependence, needed and interpreted almost as a good-night blessing. It was late when Mama turned to him, waved a hand in tired resignation, and whispered, "Papa is no more. Go to bed." Tom ran his hand over her cheek and went off to spend a confused, sleepless night. He felt lost without Papa, but somehow he knew his mother suffered even more.

Time passed, and now Mama was sick. Tom knew it was serious because Nina had arrived once again. Her presence brought on memories of the days when he was bigger than she, when Papa would send him to walk her to grammar school. How good it felt to have her tiny hand in his, as they came to a crossing. Then, as a goodbye, he would gently caress her soft cheek, as he left her safe on the school playground.

Now, Nina was all grown up, and actually, he liked it better that way, because she could provide for him, especially since it was frighteningly clear that today Mama could not.

Tom knew that in the past his mother had always been there, willing and able to please everyone. In the times when Papa lived, she had made sure that both he and Tom received just what they wanted and needed. Now, she could not come to the kitchen, and a longing tugged at Tom, as he yearned for the togetherness he had felt with both of his parents.

As he sat and rocked, Tom recalled how, because his mother was not very tall and could not reach the clothesline very well, Papa would send him out to help. Tom enjoyed their system, which was more like a ritual, really: While she shook out each item, he would get the clothespins ready. Mama would hand him each piece neatly, just as it needed to be hung, and Tom would place it on the line and attach the pins. That way, Mama did not have to stretch and risk falling.

He went on to remember the peaceful after-breakfast routine when Papa would sit beside the radio to listen to the news, while Mama settled in the chair at the dining room window. Tom would bring her the prayer book and rosary that he knew she would want. He did not know why, but he liked to watch as she turned the pages, as she whispered the words and gently fingered the beads. He listened intently for the final amen, his signal to return the book and rosary to the bedroom table.

Now, Tom could not control the flow of memories, and he longed for the times when Mama would call him as if eager to send him on an errand into the next room. He had felt needed on those occasions. Because he knew Mama's legs always hurt, he was always sure to answer her call. Oh, how disgusted he would pretend to be when, sometimes, she greeted him with a playful, "Come close. I just want to give you a kiss."

For some time now, Mama had not wanted to play. Tom had noticed, and today he yearned to see her eyes dance again in that peaceful happiness and gentle teasing.

This particular morning, however, had been a tiring one for the eighty-year-old widow lying still in the adjoining room. She had returned home from a hospital stay and was still recovering from two broken ribs in a body that ached more from eighteen months of widowhood than from the effects of a fall on the floor of the very room where her daughter now prepared lunch. There had been no time for shopping, and Nina wondered what to present that would be nourishing yet appealing to her mother's diminished appetite. She found fresh cheese and Italian bread; that would be good together with a tomato salad, simple and cool. She knew Mama would love some fruit, but not even a few grapes were to be had. Putting off this final preparation, Nina turned her attention to her brother's lunch in hopes that an inspiration would somehow come to her.

Tom had continued rocking slowly, staring fixedly at his sister, and expressing his thoughts in low, gossipy tones: "I know. Sure, I know. Nina is fixing Mama's lunch. She'll give me some, too, but she can't find fruit for Mama. Sure, I know."

"Tom, come eat your lunch. I'm going into the bedroom."

He rose, looked at Mama's tray, squeezed Nina's arm, caressed her cheek, and headed toward the back door. Puzzled by her brother's actions, Nina watched from the kitchen window and saw Tom reach up into the fig tree in the backyard. Papa had planted the tree years earlier, and though it had produced both full and lean yields, somehow their father had always managed to harvest a good supply. He had relished outwitting the ever-ready birds by hiding the new, green fruit in small paper bags lightly clipped onto the branches with Mama's clothespins. This present season, the crop was particularly sparse, but Tom had carried on in his father's memory.

Reappearing in the kitchen, Tom placed a plump, tender, moist fig on Mama's tray and set the small paper bag and clothespin beside his plate. He looked at Nina, slipped in at the table, and murmured, "I know. Sure, I know."

Natalina C. Rodriguez

This story was first published twenty years ago as "Gentle Love" in *The Cathedral Times*, the newspaper of Cathedral Parish of St. Augustine, Augustine, Florida.

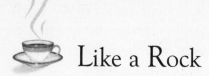 Like a Rock

My son turns to me when the judge finally speaks.

"I'll let you take him home. Do you want custody?"

"No."

He turns pale, and I feel him trembling next to me. Hurt and fear reflect in his eyes. He is too stunned to notice tears sliding down his cheeks. At fourteen, he hears only rejection, and to him, my decision means I don't love him. I know nothing I say will help. His pain cuts through me like a knife, and my tears overflow. Then, a metal door clangs loudly, and he's gone.

What have I done? He is my youngest child. Handsome and smart, his life could be all happiness and success. Why this?

I struggle to concentrate on the reasons I'm inflicting this pain on both of us. My son is already six feet tall and 180 pounds. He's challenging authority and ignoring rules. His legal transgressions emphasize the need for supervision and professional counseling. As a single mother, I cannot offer those things while providing for him. My choices are limited.

He looks older than fourteen, and he attracts older people. He's big, daring, and confused about many things, but he's young in years and experience. The possibilities of the harm that might come to him terrify me. Mental images of my child, barely into his teens, spending his remaining youth in an adult correction facility are equally frightening. If he continues to get into trouble, he will be charged as an adult.

I know I will blame myself if he gets injured or killed, or if he does something so terrible that he ends up in prison, because I failed to take action. I must try anything and everything to change his direction.

After our day in court, I pace the floor through endless nights, asking myself the same questions over and over: Did I make the best decision? Will he ever understand and forgive me? Can I live with my decision if he never comes home?

There are no answers. No way to be sure I've made the right choices. No guarantee my decisions will help my son. No comfort as I face the possibility I've lost my youngest child by trying to help him. Right or wrong, the burden is mine alone.

My head is exploding, and the ache in my chest

is unbearable. I'm physically ill from worry and heart-ache. Though I firmly believe his welfare and his future must be my priorities, nothing prepared me for this. For months, I function robotically on the verge of total exhaustion.

Every visitation day, I spend every minute I'm allowed with my son. And every visit he asks me why I don't want him.

My only positive emotional support comes from his teachers and counselors. I cling to their encouragement and advice: He has to learn where his choices lead. He has to remember and care enough not to make poor choices again. He has to take the consequences of his decisions now; he may not get a second chance. I know they are right, but every day feels like a year and time seems to crawl. The first two months feel like an eternity.

Now, when I visit, his eyes look clear and his complexion is a healthy pink. And, he admits, he feels better. The structured, secure environment doesn't allow him to walk away from responsibilities. He makes decisions and receives instant feedback. Daily living guidelines are similar to rules and routines at home, but rules are consistently enforced with logical consequences. Regular meals, chores, personal care, study time, and recreation fill the daily schedule. He still doesn't understand, but I feel a growing conviction that my decision was right.

Finally, the day arrives for him to come home. I can barely contain my happiness. I want to believe the nightmare is over, and I work hard to fill our first few days with fun. Then, my hope for a smooth transition is crushed when I discover our relationship will not be easily mended. The little boy inside the young man carries a grudge, and he never misses an opportunity to remind me how much I hurt him. I don't blame him, but his attitude limits communication.

When his eighteenth birthday passes with no sign of change in his bitter feelings toward me, I find myself facing another dilemma. Now, he is legally responsible for himself and free to make his own decisions, no longer bound by parental rules or consequences. Will I continue to endure emotionally charged challenges, or will I get on with my life and let him make his own way? I need to be there for him, but I don't need to allow him to live in the same house. Now, I have to find a way to tell him, and I already know nothing I say will be right.

My mind replays the torment of the unknown future I've been living since that day in court. I feel I'm repeating the same scene in different movies over and over.

He is angry, but he moves. At first, he flounders, and I wonder whether I'm doing the right thing. Finally, he settles on a direction.

Our relationship smoothes out after he finds a

job, rents an apartment, and starts college. The busy schedule and new responsibilities occupy his mind. He doesn't have to come to see me, but he does. Now, we laugh and talk. Our words are cautious and our emotions guarded, but I feel tremendous hope at any sign that he has not shut me out forever.

Positive changes come faster after he marries. As a young husband, he faces new responsibilities and begins to recognize my role as an adult. His attitude softens noticeably when his son is born. Witnessing his son's birth instantly adds a new dimension to his experience. The next day, he hugs me and tells me he understands a new part of my feelings as a mother.

Still, he won't talk openly about my earlier decisions and his feelings. He isn't ready to let the barrier down, but my hopes for our future rise a little higher.

During the next few years, he endures numerous challenges—divorce, losing a home, job loss, remarriage, blending families, buying a new home, and another childbirth. All add new levels of adult experiences. I also remarry during those years.

My new husband loves and accepts my family. As a result, he and my son quickly form a strong relationship. We are there for him emotionally, physically, and financially, sharing with him the joy and pain of those years, as he grows and evolves into a strong, intelligent man.

At the age of thirty-three, he is the father of three

children in a blended family. As those children grow up, the parenting challenges are increasing. His two preteen boys test limits more often and more openly. Naturally, we talk about children during most phone calls.

One day, during a pause in our conversation, he says, "Thank you for not taking me home."

My first reaction is disbelief. Gradually, I realize that the subject of our conversation hit home. His nephew, a teenager nearing his fourteenth birthday, made a poor choice that almost resulted in serious legal consequences.

I'm afraid to believe he is saying what I've wanted to hear for so many years. My response is a weak attempt at a light, teasing comeback: "You mean it worked?"

"Yeah. I don't know where I would have ended up if you hadn't done that," he said.

Suddenly, the weight I've carried for nineteen years lifts. I'm glad he can't see my smile or the tears filling my eyes. "I love you, honey."

"Love you too, Ma. Good night."

Penny J. Leisch

Rockn Da Nose

I am fortunate to be the mother of three wonderful sons. I adore my boys, but if I said I completely understood them, I would be lying. At times I've found it best just to accept them for who they are, no matter how confusing that might be. And believe me, there are aspects of their personalities that leave me bewildered—yet oddly proud. Take, for instance, the drive they all seem to have had, at some point, to shove things up their noses.

The other day as I cleared the breakfast table, my two-year-old, Raphael, walked up to me, sniffing vigorously.

"Rockn da nose," he stated.

"What, honey?"

"Rockn da nose." Sniff, sniff.

I looked at him, puzzled. *Did he just say he has a rock in his nose?*

I picked him up and stood him on the table—much to his delight. He's not allowed to stand on the table, although he's often convinced that he has a good reason to do that very thing. He looked around, pleased. He was probably wondering if this meant the unreasonable "no throwing things at your brothers" rule would also be repealed.

I tilted his head back and peered up his nose. I couldn't see anything, so I scrounged up a flashlight. The only flashlight I could find was Raphael's cow flashlight, which moos when you turn it on. So the cow and I had a look up Raphael's little snub nose. Sure enough. Rockn da nose. A little bright white rock was glistening from within the depths of his nose.

The cow mooed.

I sighed.

Last week he had put a sticker up his nose. Tomorrow . . . I don't know, probably the cat or something. For some reason, when my boys are two they seem to have a compulsion to put things up their noses. When my middle son, Max, was two, I glanced at him one day and was startled to see him looking . . . strange.

Closer inspection revealed that he had wedged two pennies in his nose, one in each nostril. They were perpendicular from his face, causing his nose to jut out unnaturally.

"Owie," he said matter-of-factly.

Indeed. What I couldn't understand is why he

would have worked so hard to achieve this look. It can't have been a comfortable process. There seems to be something in a little boy's brain that spies small objects and thinks, "Hey, I know just the place to put those! My nose!"

I remember when my oldest son, Tre, was two. One day my mom was watching him while I was out. When I came home, Mom was sitting on the floor next to Tre, with a stricken look on her face. It seems they had been playing with dried beans. I don't know why. I've found my children have a bizarre effect on my parents. Pretty much anything they ask for, my parents seriously consider giving them. So, say I walk into the room and discover Mom giving one of the boys a marshmallow 4.5 seconds before dinner; I'll give her the raised eyebrow of questioning, and she'll look back at me helplessly and protest, "But he wanted it!"

Anyhow, apparently Tre wanted to play with beans that day, and what Tre wants, Grandma delivers. Together they'd sorted beans, poured beans from cup to cup, run their fingers through great piles of beans, and generally had a grand old bean time. By the time they were done, the beans were all over the floor. So Mom had gotten out the vacuum, only to discover that our vacuum mainly just flung the beans all over the living room, with great clatters and pings.

"It was like shrapnel," she said. She started hand-collecting beans, and at one point she looked at Tre, who was "helping," and said, "Now, don't put one of these up your nose."

So, she was sort of right when she said it was her fault Tre had a bean wedged in his nostril. She was fretting that we might have to take him to the emergency room to get it out before it started to swell and cause damage to his sinuses, or something like that.

I walked up to Tre, plugged his unobstructed nostril, and said, "Blow, honey."

Well, it worked six years ago, and it still works today. Just as his big brother shot the bean out of his nose way back then, so did Raphael shoot the rock out of his nose.

I'm so proud.

I don't understand, but I'm proud.

Kira Hardison

Tender Is the Night

My teenage son had a crying spell last night. Not an unusual thing for girls, friends with daughters tell me. An argument or missed phone call triggers an outburst, and they recount a day's worth of faux pas and petty humiliations that make life at this moment unlivable. They heave their misery like poisoned food, loudly, dramatically, desperate to purge until there is not one tear left. And then, dawn breaks over a new sky, and there is hope again. It's like that, their mothers say, several times a week at worst.

I have only sons. They are sensitive, for boys, and can be emotional. But when adolescence descended on them, it came with a blackout curtain. And the worries and wonders they used to share at bedtime became private matters.

Boys are easier, I hear, as teenagers. Less histrionic. More independent. Steadier. That's true, I think, from my one-sided parenting experience. But it's deceptive, this face of self-containment. From all appearances, life is good. My son gets passing grades. He has a delightful girlfriend whose presence softens him. He actually enjoys school for once. He mountain bikes with buddies on the weekend and comes home mud splattered and endorphin charged.

But there's a bravado to him now. He carries it like a polished shield. I see him pumping it up in the car ride to school. The leather jacket. The spiked cherry-red hair. The earrings. The slouch. The tight jaw. All accoutrements to the image he hones. His voice is deeper when he grunts goodbye.

I imagine high school as a mass of projected self-images, sparring and jostling in the halls, desperately shielding the ghost children behind them. Newly sprouted fears and insecurities are snatched like plunder if exposed. It's a matter of survival, regardless of gender, to get through a day ego intact. We all did it, growing up. With luck, by senior year you've found a niche. An interest, a passion—or, if nothing else, a clique—to foster confidence and growth. You come out the other end with a stronger sense of self.

My son is just a freshman, struggling with the hardest part: trying to figure out who it is he wants to be seen as, before he can get to the part about who he really is. And I don't get to help. At least not in ways I normally consider helpful. Questions are considered intrusions, embraces are assaults, family time is a bore. I've learned to give him a wide berth and take the openings when I see them. I feel gratitude for the smallest things: a smile flashed my way at the funny part in a video, an unexpected hug while I make dinner, an unprompted thank-you. Mostly, I simply have to take at face value the side he shows to me, because the rest is inaccessible.

But last night he called out from his bed, where he lay crying, unable to stop. He held out his arms and clung tight like he hasn't for years. An earring had started it. A garnet stud swirled down the bathroom drain. It triggered an avalanche in him that stymied us both.

"Is there something else?" I asked. "Something that's been bothering you? What's going on?"

"I just need to cry," he wailed. "I need to get it all out. It's not fair how I never get to cry anymore. All day at school, I walk around holding it in."

I thought he liked school. "Is it that bad? Is someone hurting you?" I envisioned a bully by the lockers twisting his arm, gangs of ruffians surrounding him at the bus stop after school. What undisclosed maliciousness had been tormenting him?

"No, it's not any *thing*. It's just the way it is. You have to be tough all the time. If you start to feel something that isn't cool, you have to hide it."

I remembered how upset he'd been when his

class watched a movie that showed wild animals being killed and someone in the room had cheered when the elephant was brought down. How furious he'd been when a classmate once suggested that all retarded people should be euthanized.

He let out a long, thin wail and rolled his head from side to side. "It feels like a balloon getting blown up inside of me. All these feelings. I can't ever let them out. Not with my friends. And at school, you're dead meat if you cry. Even if you're really hurt bad."

It's true. High school is a cruel Darwinian society, and the weakest are smeared. I remember seeing a boy taunted to tears in my own high school, and it was like watching someone being handed a death sentence. Everyone knew. There was no coming back from this. I didn't know what to tell my son, except, "You're right. You have to hold it in. But when you're home and safe, let it out, and we'll be here with you."

I remembered him coming home the previous weekend, his leg bloody from biking. A friend was with him, and he brandished that sheared shin like a trophy, bragging about how deep it cut and how little it hurt. Only after his friend left would he let me bandage it. He swung his leg up on the kitchen table, still full of swagger and talk. And I thought how far he had grown from the little boy who wanted kisses and a *Jurassic Park* Band-Aid for every little scratch and bruise. *Growing up*, I'd thought. *Tougher than me now.*

But last night I was grateful for the chance to hold him again. To pat down his stiff red hair and wipe his tears. To feel the bird-thin bones beneath new muscle and realize, *My God, he's still such a kid.*

You forget, when they peer smugly down at you from gangly new legs. They bang their way around the kitchen making meals you never knew they could cook. They can get themselves all around town without asking for a ride. They don't come to you for advice, and snap at you if you offer it. It's easy, then, to think you've reached the downhill part, that most of the lessons you've taught already, and this is your time to coast. You leave him alone when he doesn't want to talk and believe him when he says he's okay. You remember things you forgot to do, like learn Italian and write a book. And you think that maybe the time has come at last for you to focus on yourself and your child-weary partnership.

But really, this is the trickiest part of all. They want you there, right next to them, when they need you—knowing all the right things to do and say. And then . . . *poof!* The distance barrier inflates like an airbag, and you find yourself dumped on your ass, wondering what it was you said or did.

I'm left navigating a million double-messages, trying to distinguish real boundaries from false fronts, poking the ground for hidden passages. I stumble against my own needs and insecurities, never sure how my advances will be received. But I'm the mom, and it's up to me to read the signals, take the chances, and absorb the blows if my timing was off or the angle was wrong.

No doubt he will come home from school today more gruff and disinterested than ever (just to make sure I don't get any ideas about last night). But I'm reminded now that behind that fifteen-year-old façade, my child still lingers, and no matter how deftly he dodges connection, he still counts on me to know when to come in there after him. And as much as I hate that he has things to cry about, I love that he still cries.

Jennifer Meyer

To the Bat Cave, Mama!

When I was a young boy, I wanted to change my name to "Batman." "Thomas Batman Smith" had a nice ring to it. Much better than my original choice: "Thomas Batman Bruce Wayne Smith." That seemed a little pretentious, even at age seven.

Batman was a perfectly logical choice as a new name for a child of the sixties. Especially one who had a Batman lunch box, a Batman notebook, Batman stickers, tons of Batman comic books, a Batman license plate for his bicycle, and a genuine autographed picture of the Caped Crusader himself.

It was during this name-changing frenzy that the world changed. A friend of mine saw it on television on a Sunday night, and by Monday morning, every student at Aurelian Springs School. Batman was going to be on TV. In his own show. And not just once, but *twice* each week.

Could life get any better?

All I had to do was tune in to the right bat-network on the right bat-night, and my life would be perfect.

"I don't know about that."

Oh Lord, there it was. The voice of doom. The one teeny little problem with the plan. The one thing with the power to end my bat-universe before it ever had a chance to unfold. Mama's voice.

Now, don't get me wrong. I love my mama. I've known her all my life. And she is one of the kindest, most thoughtful, self-sacrificing examples of mother-hood I've ever seen. But up to that point in her life, she had never read a Batman comic book, never plastered Batman stickers all over her notebook, and never run around the playground with the sleeves of her windbreaker tied around her neck like a cape, chasing Gene "The Riddler" Cobb.

(To be fair, though, she did not laugh when I got the plastic cape of my Batman Halloween costume caught between the back tire and fender of my bike and sailed over backward on takeoff that one time.)

Still, those words struck terror into my heart: *I don't know about that.* Could she be serious? How could you not know about watching Batman on TV? Especially twice a week!

"Let me think about it."

That was a death knell if ever there was one. (She's still thinking about buying me a minibike, thirty-six years after that "let me think about it" episode.) I knew I had to think fast.

"But, Mama, we have to watch it. It's Batman. The one I dressed up like on Halloween. He's a good guy. And a super hero," I said with unerring second-grader logic.

"I know that," she said, "but it might be too scary."

"It won't be scary," I reasoned with mental agility rivaling that of Plato, Winston Churchill, and Captain Kangaroo combined. "He doesn't kill people. He just takes them to jail in the Batmobile."

"We'll see."

After some all-out pleading (it was obvious logic wasn't going to help), she said, "I'll tell you what; I'll watch it with you, but if it gets too scary, I'm going to turn it."

That very week, what started out as a mother watching out for the little fellow she brought into the world turned into something we did together twice a week. While she sat on the couch doing schoolwork (my mom is a teacher), I sat on the couch secretly being Batman.

Time passed. The Caped Crusader visited our home twice a week, regular as clockwork. And the calendar gradually moved toward October. November. Then the big one: December.

From the sound of things, when my parents went to see Santa in November (somehow they always met him in Richmond right after Thanksgiving), he was going to have a pretty packed sleigh when he hit our house. I know, because my Christmas list was probably two pages long.

What I didn't know back then was that a preacher and a first-year teacher didn't make much money, and they had to save a long time to visit Santa's lay-away department and make that final payment on a sack full of Christmas cheer. They did without things they wanted so they could see the light in their sons' eyes. My brother and I wouldn't know these things for years.

What I did know that year, however—long after Santa had turned our Christmas cache over to Mama and Daddy—was that there was a new item in the Sears catalog. The granddaddy of all treasures. A real Batman suit. Not a plastic mask and nylon cape. But a real fabric costume. Complete with cowl and ears.

Holy Christmas Jitters!

I think I must have asked, begged, and pleaded nonstop for a week, but to no avail. Santa had already done everything he could. That was the sad news.

"We've already seen Santa Claus, and we don't have a way to get a letter to him in time," Mama said. "Maybe he can bring you one next year."

I wanted that suit as much as some folks want world peace, but I knew when to quit. So I said, "Okay," and prepared for a disappointing Christmas.

Every day brought Christmas one day closer, and sprinkled in among the evergreen boughs, mugs of hot chocolate with marshmallows, and Mel Torme singing, "Chestnuts roasting on an open fire . . . ," was one occasional question.

"Are you sure Santa won't be able to bring that Batman suit?"

The answer was always the same.

"I'm afraid not. Not this year. Maybe next year."

What a disappointed little fellow with visions of fighting crime and watching TV twice a week in style didn't understand was that sometimes the money just isn't there. And sometimes a mother has to say no.

But even a major disappointment can be held in check when the temperature drops, the Christmas lights shine on the tree, and the radio plays nothing but Yuletide melodies. As I recall, that Christmas morning started out pretty good as the wrapping paper started flying, as shiny new cap pistols cracked, and as long red stockings gave up their bounty. Though I would have loved to see a real Batman costume laid out on the couch where the cowboy hat and guns had been, I understood that was not to be.

Mama walked over and said, "Well, was Santa good to you?"

Boy, oh boy! Even without the prize of all prizes, Santa had done himself proud. A football, some cow-boy stuff, a lot of books, and a paint-by-numbers set.

A pretty fine Christmas haul by any standard

"Here," she said and handed me a box. "Santa left this in my presents by mistake. It has your name on it."

You guessed it. I opened the box and there, in all its bat-glory, was a real Batman costume. Made out of real fabric, with a real Batman emblem on the chest, a real cape, a real cowl with bat ears, and a real fabric utility belt.

The thing you haven't guessed—and the thing I didn't know until I was grown—was that my mother made that Batman suit. She would slip over to Grandmamma and Granddaddy's house whenever she could and work on it. My grandmamma helped her with it some, but mostly it was my mother. Working late at night. Sewing a Batman costume with only a catalog picture as a pattern. Showing her little boy that if you wish hard enough, your Christmas dreams can come true. And teaching her grown son that sometimes love is a tangible thing.

Thomas Smith

Out of the Darkness

"I know he's in there somewhere," I mumbled, my voice thick with fatigue. I heard laughter in the room, and someone said, "Well, he's certainly taking his time."

It was 1978, and I was trying to deliver my third baby in four years. This one should have fallen out effortlessly. Instead, I had been in labor for twenty-two hours. I imagined this baby hiding in the quiet darkness deep inside of me, not wanting to come out to face the risks of living. And then I thought of him as lost, desperate, clawing his way out to the edge of being.

"Now, breathe with me," the nurse nearest me instructed. "One . . . two . . . three . . ."

I mirrored her breaths, fixing my eyes on the bright light above my head.

"Okay, good. Now, blow out and push."

Exhausted, I struggled to bring this child into our

family, to make him know where he belonged, how he belonged, and to whom he belonged.

"Relax for a minute," the nurse said before leaning in close to me as if eager to share a secret. "So, I'm curious. How do you know it's a boy?"

Through a foggy mind and parched lips I whispered one word: "Drano."

This was our surprise baby, the unplanned one. Although my husband's love for our two daughters was infinite, I suspected he yearned for a son, a shadow of himself. Any doubts I had about this were laid to rest one evening in the sixth month of my pregnancy when he came home carrying a paper bag, breathless with excitement.

"I heard about this on the radio," he began, removing his coat and holding up the paper bag.

"About what?" I asked.

He reached into the bag and pulled out a can of Drano. "They say you can tell the sex of the baby by spitting into crystal Drano."*

"You've got to be kidding! What does Drano have to do with—"

"Go ahead, try," he interrupted. By then, he'd reached the kitchen and poured the blue crystals into a saucer.

"But . . ."

"Come on, just try it," he insisted, holding the saucer under my chin.

"Okay," I laughed, "but this seems crazy!"

I spat. The Drano sizzled and turned from pale blue to black.

"Yes! Yes!" he shouted, as he bounced around the kitchen, hands held high as if he had scored the winning touchdown.

"What just happened?" I stared at him across the kitchen.

"The guy on the radio said that if the Drano turns black, it's a boy," my husband said, beaming, "and it turned black!"

"Well, what do you know," I said, sounding unconvinced. I didn't know how to tell him that I had the intuition from the beginning of my pregnancy that I was carrying a son. Without tests or gimmicks or other rational support, there was no doubt in my heart that we were having a son.

Three months later, the rhythmic, mechanical pulse of a fetal monitor interrupted the quiet in a delivery room crowded with gowned and masked figures wearing paper shoes that muffled their footsteps on the tile floor.

"Give me one good push," a voice insisted.

I grudgingly obliged and felt a tremendous heaviness followed by the urge to sleep forever. An anxious stillness gripped the room, a moment of held breaths, waiting. And then I heard the air fill with the sounds of new life.

"It's a boy," someone announced.

"I told you he was in there somewhere," I laughed, numb with joy. "This one's for my husband."

"Oh, no, boys are for their mothers," the nurse nearest me whispered.

I was too exhausted to do anything but smile and sleep.

My hand touches the glass on the sixth-floor waiting-room window. It is 1993, not quite eight in the morning, and the window feels warm. Another hot May day. I am reliving the moment of my son's birth, uncovering each moment like hoarded treasure. The nurse had been right: Boys are for their mothers. I have so many images of him, stored in my memory like clothes arranged in an antique trunk. I unfold them, layer by layer, determined that by remembering I will keep him alive.

My son, Dale Sorlie Ness Jr., now fourteen years old, lies in the neurosurgical intensive care unit of a local hospital. Seven days earlier, he'd joined three other boys in a nearby park to practice baseball. He was the pitcher when his best friend, Ricky, came up to bat. Dale went with the fastball, and Ricky went for the home run. The ball shot from the bat, destined by its speed to fly far over the outfield fence. But it was low, too low. Dale saw it coming and tried to duck. The ball slammed into the left side of his head, fracturing his skull and setting off a chain of events that left his brain swollen and bruised.

In the first hours after the accident, his memory deteriorated as the condition of his brain worsened. Recalling simple facts, such as the date, his home address, and his sisters' names, became increasingly difficult for him.

Determined to help him hold on to his memory, we filled his hospital room with what mattered most to him: pictures of his eighth-grade teammates, of his dog, and of a recent Easter together as a family. But our grasp was slippery, and he continued to lose memory, speech, and the use of his right arm. He slid into unconsciousness, what seemed like a bottomless black hole. The decision was made to move him to the ICU.

Today, after six days in the ICU, his condition remains unchanged. We are allowed to visit him every three hours for ten minutes, from nine in the morning until nine in the evening. Each visit becomes an opportunity to see him alive again, his eyes closed, his very being distant and unreachable.

My habit is to move beyond the tubes and wires, to find the boy that I know is in there somewhere, fighting to find his way out of that darkness. I realize how long it has been since I have really looked at him. His fourteen-year-old frame stretches along the bed, his long, thin bones taking on a man's shape. But his face still looks young, his skin smooth and soft, no sign of a man's pain or world-weariness.

Taking his hand, I notice his fingernails, uneven and dirty, and I wonder out loud, "How long has it been since he cut these?" I marvel at the layers of dirt under the nails and how much this dirt says about him: sand from our backyard, picked up as he dug for balls to throw to his dog, Katie; dark, rich dirt and scraps of grass from the school field shoved under his nails when he dove for a ball in the infield; red clay from the pitcher's mound at Woodland Park, where he worked his hand around the ball, preparing for the perfect fastball or curve.

At each visit I try to think of a memory to share, whispering my monologue while stroking his hand or face, dropping words into the silence like Gretel's bread crumbs, hoping to lead him home.

"You were such a fussy baby. In the middle of every night, you would wake me up and I would have to dance around with you, singing again and again, 'Nothing you can say could tear me away from my guy.'"

I want him to remember where he belongs, how he belongs, to whom he belongs. "And I'll never forget your first no-hitter, just six weeks ago, on my birthday. I kept my eyes squeezed shut through the last inning, certain I would jinx you if I looked at the pitches, but also just as certain you could do it and I could help by imagining every pitch going into the strike zone. After the last strikeout, you ran off the mound, past your cheering teammates, right up to the fence, and threw me the ball. 'Happy Birthday, Mom,' you said. And I cried."

I want him to know that, if he is lost and desperate, I will help him claw his way back to the edge of being.

Most of the time, my husband and I keep a vigil in the waiting room. Hope hangs like fog, heavy with the prayers and visits of friends, yet quick to evaporate when we reach out to grasp it. Fighting to keep our lives from disintegrating, we talk little to each other, a conspiracy of silence that provides protection from our deepest fears. I wonder if my son will ever wake up. If he does wake up, I wonder who he will be and what or whom he will remember. I cling to my mother's intuition, the same one that told me he would be a boy, the one that tells me now he will return from the darkness.

As another day ends, I find my husband by the waiting-room window, staring into the night. We are sad and quiet, the silence between us thick with the sense that someone has been recently removed and his presence still hangs here. My husband agrees to go home to spend the night with our daughters. I agree to stay, in case there is any change in Dale's condition.

Morning arrives. I stand by the waiting-room window, watching the wind sweep across the hospital parking lot, sifting through piles of trash, lifting the edge of a construction tarp, searching. A line of cars stops at the hospital entrance, dispensing people hurrying to their daily routines. Life goes on, and I am suddenly saddened by its indifference.

The waiting room phone rings. The only person there, I answer it.

"This is Jane Ness."

"Mrs. Ness, this is Mark, the night nurse, back in the ICU."

"Oh, good morning, Mark. Any news?"

"We need you to come back here right away."

My hand tightens on the phone, and I hesitate, suddenly paralyzed with fear.

"Mrs. Ness, are you still there?"

"Yes, I'm here," I manage to respond. "I should call my husband."

"I need you to come now, Mrs. Ness. This can't wait."

"Is something wrong?" I begin, but Mark has already hung up.

I call my husband, but he doesn't answer. I head to the ICU alone.

"God, please," I whisper, hurrying down the silent hallway, "I'll do anything, anything, please. Don't let him . . . please."

I feel lightheaded and realize I am holding my breath.

"Breathe," I tell myself, and I begin to count out loud, "One . . . two . . . three . . . in, out, slowly."

My heart pounds as I round the corner and push through the ICU door.

Overwhelmed by the monotonous mechanical pulses of machines supporting fragile lives not yet gone, I feel suddenly numb, exhausted, unprepared. Dale's cubicle is to the right of the door. I force myself to move past the curtain in front of it.

In that instant, I notice his eyes—open and fixed on me.

"Hey, Dale, someone's here to see you." I hear Mark's voice to my right.

My eyes remain locked on Dale's eyes, and I watch him struggle to break through some barrier in his mind, to bring himself back to where he belongs. An anxious stillness grips the room, a moment of held breaths, waiting, hoping. Dale's voice shatters the silence. It is weak, but the word is unmistakable.

"Mom."

The air fills with this sound of new life. My mind is mute. Only my heart can speak.

"I knew that you were in there somewhere."

Jane Ness

---

*Studies have shown that fetal gender cannot be determined by spitting or urinating into Drano and that direct contact with these products can pose health risks to pregnant women and their unborn children.

A Date to Remember

It was my first evening out with a member of the opposite sex in nearly two years.

As the handsome, dark-haired, brown-eyed guy gazed at me from across the dining table, his wide grin immediately put me at ease. Having been a widow for several years and having experienced two failed relationships since my husband's death, I had decided to forego dating and to focus totally on myself and my two young sons. Most of my weekends were spent at the boys' sporting events or watching Friday evening videos and eating pizza together. Sometimes, they both slept over at friends' homes, and I'd choose to stay in alone, feeling sorry for myself.

This Friday-night outing was a big step for me. I realized I needed a break from my normal routine, and this person was, for myriad reasons, an ideal choice for a dinner companion. Glancing at him as he perused the menu and continued to smile at me, I had a feeling this was going to be an enjoyable evening.

I was not disappointed.

After we placed our orders, my date surprised me by moving to my side of the table, where he sat next to me in a very gentlemanly manner. He asked a lot of questions about my workday and about the family vacation I was planning. He really shocked me when he unfolded my napkin for me and tenderly placed it on my lap. Having never experienced a guy sitting next to me or taking care of my napkin, I was a bit taken aback, yet I was eager to see how the night might unfold (no pun intended).

Upon leaving the shopping-mall–based eatery, I asked my companion if he would accompany me to the perfume store. I fully expected to see a grimace on his face, so I was pleasantly surprised when he broke into a bright smile and enthusiastically replied, "Sure!" As I sampled numerous fragrances in the well-stocked shop, my date started selecting various scents he thought I'd like, playfully spraying them on my wrists, neck, and hair. We sampled, teased, laughed, and coughed for several minutes, evoking some pretty strange looks from the salespeople. Although we left the store without making a single purchase, an aromatic breeze trailed us, a scented reminder of the fun I was having—and the evening was still young.

A guy who is patient and humorous while a

woman tests cologne just might be agreeable to accompanying her on a quest for a new coat. My date was not only amenable, he was downright commendable. Making himself comfortable in a cushy chair, he watched me model the coats I liked. He seemed really interested, too, as he gave his opinions on my choices and sat contentedly while I made a decision. He even applauded my buy, commenting to the salesclerk how nice I looked in it. This young man definitely had an eye for style, and he was certainly different in many ways from my previous dates.

Because we were having such a fine time together, we decided to visit a science-oriented store, one of those places that allow customers to play with its displayed gadgetry. Rhett, my date, was able to coax the child in me into trying nearly every item. He eagerly peered into a kaleidoscope, exclaiming, "Wow!" Passing the tube to me, he instructed me on how to turn it to see the different designs, as I wondered how many guys would take the time to do that.

We giggled and joked in the science store just as we had in the perfume shop. We laughed so much and so hard, at times we could barely stand and tears flowed from my eyes. The high point of the excursion was when Rhett tested one of those snowboarding simulators that are used with a television. Though I was quite impressed with his balance on the swaying board, neither of us could contain our laughter the few times he fell, each time making some goofy face. This guy's sense of humor and his ability to laugh at himself impressed me so much.

We casually browsed in a few more shops before we chose to end our mall adventure at Starbucks. Settling into large armchairs, we sipped lattes and talked about our evening together, agreeing it was the best time either of us had spent in recent months. After we chatted a bit, Rhett bought a cookie for us to share, and we sat quietly, enjoying our refreshments and being together. Three hours had passed much too quickly.

As we headed toward the parking garage, Rhett surprised me when he reached for my hand. He held it firmly while we walked in silence toward our car. He appeared tired, but as we approached the vehicle, he turned to me and said, "I had a really nice time tonight. Let's do this again soon."

"Ditto," I answered as we got into the car.

Rhett was right. It had been a very nice evening.

Driving home, I thought about the incredible joy I'd discovered in my few hours with this guy. We had a wonderful dinner, we played, and we shared conversation over coffee. Our time together far surpassed my usual Friday night, spent at home by myself or doing the pizza-and-video routine. Rhett showed me I could actually spend an evening out and enjoy it, that I could even act somewhat silly in public and laugh until tears streamed down my face.

Indeed, tears trickled down my cheeks as I continued to reflect on my time with this special guy. Looking over at my sleeping son in the passenger seat, I recalled the many times he'd commented, "Mom, you need to get out for a night. I'll take you on a date." On this particular day, I had finally accepted his offer (although I paid the evening's expenses), and I was delighted to discover that hanging out with my ten-year-old son was a pretty great thing. There and then, I vowed to have a "date" with my growing child as frequently as possible, knowing that in a few years he would probably no longer want to take his mom for an evening on the town.

In the years that followed, Rhett and I enjoyed many wonderful times together, and we still occasionally go out to dinner, just the two of us. He's now a teenager with a hectic sports and social schedule, and like most teens, he usually prefers spending time with his friends over spending time with his mom. Still, I hope he will always remember the fun we had together that winter's night at the mall, though I suspect his memories have faded in the midst of soccer, football, and girls. That's reality. But in his mother's heart and mind, it will always be a date to remember.

Amy Walton

Marching Orders

"Let me go!" my teenage son, Lamont, yells at me.

I clench my jaw, determined to hold back tears.

"Let me go!" he yells even louder.

Today is the last muggy day of freshman orientation at Morehouse, a historically black, all-male college in Atlanta, Georgia.

I am new to this "college goodbye" business, and it shows. My heart is pounding, and my muscles are tense. I take deep breaths to calm myself. I never thought that letting go of my "baby"—a six-foot-one, mustached, and self-assured history major—could hurt so much.

Of course, I am proud Morehouse accepted Lamont. This campus of manicured lawns and pre-antebellum brick buildings is known worldwide as the finest institution of higher learning for African

American men. My son will walk the same cobbled pathways and take exams in the same classrooms as did civil rights leader Martin Luther King, Jr., former U.S. Ambassador Andrew Young, and film writer/ director/producer Spike Lee.

What an adventure for him. And what terror for me. I am a single mother to an only child. I will fly back to California tonight, but my entire life will remain in Georgia.

I remember when I first discovered that Lamont and I were kindred spirits. Barely out of training pants, Lamont and the four-year-old girl from next door were best friends. One day, I washed dishes as they played in the living room.

"We're gonna play house," Lamont announced.

I wiped the soap from my hands and crept to the doorway. Far be it for me to interrupt innocent child's play, but I stood ready to halt any inappropriate pre-kindergarten tryst.

"I'm the daddy," he told her. "Your job is to be quiet. I have some very important studying to do, and I can't be disturbed."

I muffled a giggle. At the time, I was enrolled in an MBA program, and so I understood the reference. I pledged to spend more time with my son, then puffed out my chest and strutted back into the kitchen. The kid was a regular chip off the old block. I was always the bespectacled brainy kid who routinely requested extra homework. Though not as nerdish as me, Lamont also takes his education seriously.

Today, I sit here in the Morehouse auditorium because of his academic hard work and determination. Though I cannot see him, I know Lamont is up front, shoulder to shoulder with more than 900 other young men, the incoming class of 2007. They fill the first twenty rows of seats, a squadron of teenagers—some looking awkward, some looking confidant—in white shirts, Windsor-knotted ties, and dark suits.

The vice president of academic affairs, a tall, regal woman in an ivory pantsuit, is on the stage. The timbre of her clear, deep voice matches the solemnity of the occasion. The ceremony reminds me of a black Baptist church service, complete with a local minister's singsong opening prayer and Bible reading followed by soulful Christian hymns sung by a Morehouse choir swaying to the beat.

The associate dean welcomes us and summarizes the past week of orientation workshops and seminars. She turns her attention to our sons.

"Class of two thousand seven, please stand."

The young men stand amid muffled squeaks of leather auditorium seats.

"Turn to face your parents and guardians," she continues.

They turn from facing the stage to facing all of us in the upper rows.

"Gentlemen, today you stand before those who have nurtured and cared for you through your young lives. These individuals supported you with love and understanding—even when you felt undeserving of such unconditional devotion." The associate dean's voice rises and falls in the syncopated rhythm of a country preacher. "They taught you right from wrong, and instilled in you the dedication, faith, and intellect that led you to gain admission to this magnificent institution, Morehouse College. Their job is done."

I feel the pinprick of tears. Several women near me sniffle.

"I now request that you tell your parents and guardians that you are ready to move on to the new opportunities and challenges ahead. Gentlemen, address your parents, repeating after me. . . .

"I . . . ," she booms.

"I . . . ," the loud, deep voices of Morehouse's class of 2007 respond.

"Now, say your name," she commands.

A roar of garbled voices rises from the group as each young man shouts his full name.

"Understand and appreciate the sacrifices you made for me . . . ," she thunders.

"Understand and appreciate the sacrifices you made for me . . . ," they echo.

"And I will make you proud . . ."

"And I will make you proud . . ."

"But for me to be all that you hope and pray for . . ."

"But for me to be all that you hope and pray for . . ."

"You must please . . ."

"You must please . . ."

"Let me go!" she shouts.

"Let me go!" Lamont yells at me from somewhere in the vast auditorium of other young men yelling at their parents.

My son is giving me permission to do what I was so afraid to do until this moment—say goodbye.

"Let me go!" the administrator repeats, this time louder.

"Let me go!" Lamont and his classmates yell louder.

She pauses and gazes into the upper reaches of the auditorium where family members sit.

"Mom, Dad, and guardians, it is your turn to stand."

We do, many in the audience wiping away tears.

"I want you to think back to when your young man was just a little boy. Remember when he got that first bicycle without training wheels and you taught him how to ride?" she asks.

Nervous laughter ripples through the auditorium, as many others and I nod our heads.

"You remember, you ran alongside of him, your

hands next to his on the handlebars while he peddled as fast as he could. After you had gone a fair distance, remember what he said to you, Mom and Dad?"

She pauses.

"He said, 'Let me go!'"

Another pause.

"He said, 'Let me go!' And you didn't want to. You were so afraid he would fall and hurt himself. But you forced yourself to let him go, anyway. He wobbled a little at first, but then he gathered balance and speed, and soon he was riding on his own."

I smile and nod my head, as do many of the care-takers around me.

"Well, now it is time to let him go again," she says in a booming voice. "Now, repeat after me. "Son . . ."

"Son . . . ," we parents and guardians repeat.

"I am so proud of you . . ."

"I am so proud of you . . ."

"And I am officially . . ."

"And I am officially . . ."

"Letting you go," she yells.

"Letting you go," the other parents and I yell.

"I am letting you go!" she yells louder.

"I am letting you go," we repeat louder.

My tears fall slowly at first, and then I am sobbing and fumbling in my purse for a tissue. I find one and blow my nose, noticing that most of the women and some of the men around me are crying, too. But the tears are ones of pride and acceptance. It feels so good to finally release the sadness that has weighed me down all week. My tears flow down my cheeks and into my huge grin.

Later that evening, Lamont and I are at the curb outside of his dormitory. My cab to the airport idles nearby. We have exhausted the "leaving home" details that I feel compelled to squeeze into our last moments together. No, he won't forget to call regularly, even if it has to be collect. Yes, he has enough quarters for the laundry. No, he doesn't think he will need a heavier coat. I hug him tightly for about a minute, a good thirty seconds longer than he would have allowed any other time.

"Bye, Lamont," I say as he closes the door of the cab for me. "I love you."

"I love you, too, Mom," he says as I roll down the window. "Goodbye."

As the cab drives off, we wave to each other. Both our faces break into wide, stupid smiles—his because of the wonderful adventures that lie ahead and mine because I finally recognize that this parting is, in fact, a good one.

Jeanette Valentine

A Prince
by Any Other Name

Fifty-five years ago, as she patiently awaited the birth of her first child, Gladys knitted a special Christmas sweater for her husband. The sweater was formed from gray wool; on its front were two brightly colored reindeer and a tall fir tree. On December twelfth, as snow softly fell from the early winter sky, her son, Rodger, came into the world. Gladys's love for him was so pure, so sweet. Whenever she changed his diapers or fed him, she gazed into his eyes and gently whispered, "You are my little prince." Often, to her husband, Cap, she would say, "Honey, he looks just like you."

Rodger was the kind of son Gladys had always dreamed of: respectful, kind, and a bit adventurous. Like many boys raised during the 1950s, he spent a great deal of his childhood outdoors, either in the woods or near the pond behind his home. On several occasions, Gladys arrived home only to be greeted by frogs and snapping turtles. School meetings, baseball games, and Boy Scout functions filled Gladys's days and evenings. Rodger grew more like his dad every day. Eventually, he wore his father's Christmas sweater, so lovingly knitted by his mom when she carried him in her womb.

At age fourteen, Rodger joined the local volunteer fire company, and his mother's heart burst with pride. Because he was too young to drive, he rode his bicycle to fire calls. He continued in the fire service as an adult, becoming president and chief of his fire department. When Rodger left during Viet Nam to serve his country in the U.S. Army, his mother cried gallons of tears as she waved him goodbye. When he safely returned home after three years of duty, she sobbed tears of joy.

Rodger met his future wife, Sue, one cold January evening, and their lives changed forever. Sue instantly fell in love with his kind manner and handsome face. They married and happily raised a family. Gladys showered her grandchildren with love; she knitted them beautiful mittens and hats. And like his father and grandfather before him, Rodger's son, Mike, grew to wear Gladys's handmade reindeer Christmas sweater.

Then, a cruel twist marred their life's journey when Gladys was diagnosed with Alzheimer's. As her memory slowly faded and she climbed deeper into the disease, her husband, Cap, patiently looked after her every day. Rodger and his sister, Dawn, admired their dad's strength but worried about his well-being, for he resisted all help in caring for his ailing wife.

Again the road turned sharply when Rodger received an urgent phone call from his dad. "Please come at once. I'm very sick."

His father was rushed to the hospital and had to undergo emergency major surgery. Rodger and his sister were faced with the difficult decision to stay and care for their mom or to place her in a nursing home during their father's hospitalization and recovery. They chose to stay for the duration. Rodger took a leave of absence from work, and he and Dawn grew closer as they moved into their parents' home. Their days were spent caring for their mom and visiting their dad in the hospital.

To afford her sister-in-law a much-needed break and the chance to return to her family, Sue traveled to be with her husband, Rodger, at his parents' home on weekends. With the lingering nearness of his mom's death and the uncertainty of his father's health, Rodger found that, for him and Sue, the things that really mattered in their lives were becoming more apparent. Sometimes they just held each other. Sue came to know her husband in a new way. She had always known that Rodger, like his dad, was a devoted son, husband, and father. But it was during his parents' illnesses that Sue first witnessed the depth of her husband's compassion, love, and devotion.

Reaching deep within his soul, Rodger found the inner strength to provide for his mother's most personal needs. He cared for her in the same tender manner in which she had cared for him as a baby. He returned to her the same pure, sweet love. Early every morning, Sue would hear Rodger say tenderly, "Hi, Mom. How are you today?" as he carefully spooned cereal into her mouth. Whenever he changed her diapers or bathed her, his touch was soft and gentle. And though his mother stared blankly and couldn't speak, Sue was quite certain that on several occasions she heard Gladys faintly whisper to Rodger, "You are my prince."

On the same day that her husband, Cap, returned home from the hospital, Gladys died. She waited for him to see her one last time. Somehow, she must have known that he wouldn't be able to take care of her anymore. In the months before her death, she drew her family closer together than they had ever been before.

I am happy to acknowledge that Rodger is my husband and Gladys was my mother-in-law. During that melancholy period in our lives, I learned something invaluable: Should I ever face mental or physical frailty, I need not worry; my husband is a prince.

Susan J. Siersma

The Other Woman

My four-year-old son, Ben, has thrown me over for another woman.

When I enrolled him in preschool last fall, I expected him to work on his fine motor development and socialization skills; I never imagined this could happen. After all, the preschool came highly recommended, and I was impressed with the teacher, Miss Linda, who had several years of experience and seemed to have a good rapport with the children.

Now, three months later, my son can write his name, has made dozens of new friends, and his self-esteem has never been higher. But Miss Linda has risen to movie star status, while I've become nothing more than another pair of outstretched hands, good only for wiping noses and slinging peanut butter and jelly sandwiches.

Oh, it all began innocently enough. I'd pick him up from preschool and he'd tell me all about his day of finger painting or coloring. My first inkling that something was amiss came when he started mentioning circle time with a faraway look in his eyes.

"Did you know Miss Linda sang us a song about a pizza?" he'd say wistfully.

At first I didn't mind. I was pleased he had adapted so well to his new school. But after a few weeks, his goodbye kisses turned into a quick hug before he bolted out of my arms toward the block area. A week later, he just casually waved goodbye from the "play dough" table across the room. I expected him to eventually stop me at the door, shake my hand, and say, "Well, I'll see you 'round sometime."

I began to worry when I noticed other signs of his infatuation. Like when he asked me why my glasses weren't round like Miss Linda's. And why I didn't double-knot his tennis shoes like Miss Linda did. Or the time he insisted I wasn't writing his name correctly on his lunch bag, reasoning, "Miss Linda doesn't make 'Bs' like that."

It was obvious I was no longer on the top of my son's A-list. My popularity had slid farther down the alphabet . . . somewhere between yams and zucchini. Now, this came as quite a shock, since only a few short months ago I was "The Smartest, Most Favorite Person in the Universe." Life was so simple then. Ben and I would spend our days at the playground, in Gymboree class, or taking nature walks around the block. He'd ask a lot of questions about things, like why birds fly or what keeps two-wheeled bikes from falling over. He even believed my answers. And if I had to leave him with a babysitter to do an errand, he'd cry, "Mommy!" and rush into my arms for a big hug when I returned.

All that is over now. In the beginning, I tried to pretend it didn't bother me. The charade didn't work. So, I did the only other thing a secure and sensible mother would do: I bought a pair of tiny oval-shaped sunglasses, worked on my penmanship, and tried to show my little guy that I could be just as wonderful as Miss Linda.

I thought I was passing the grade . . . until I made the terrible mistake of reading him a bedtime story he had already heard in preschool. Sitting on my lap as I read to him, he stopped me halfway through the first page.

"Miss Linda lets us see the pictures first," he said.

I turned the book toward him and continued reading, upside down.

"And Mom," he said. "You forgot to make the animal sounds."

Pointing at the pictures, I did my best. But where I *barked*, Miss Linda had *woofed*; where I *neighed*, she had *whinnied*; and where I *oinked*, she had definitely *snorted*.

"You're not doing it right," my son said, exasperated.

Achieving Miss Linda status was going to be much harder than I had thought. We somehow got through the rest of the story, but when I gave him a kiss and turned out the light, I heard him sigh.

The next night I decided to show my son how fun and hip I could be, and suggested we skip the story and sing silly songs, instead. This was my chance to shine; after all, I'd been singing these ditties to my children for years. But halfway through the "Itsy-Bitsy Spider," my son informed me that not only was I singing different words than Miss Linda, but I wasn't making the spider correctly with my fingers.

Things were so much easier when I was popular. Still, I must concede that being unpopular does have its perks. I don't have to worry about living up to a lofty image, I don't have to answer a lot of questions, and I have plenty of free time alone to catch up on things like crocheting and playing solitaire.

But deep down, I want back my old place in the sun. I wonder what Miss Linda has that I haven't got. At least I know my son's attraction isn't purely physical. After all, Miss Linda is middle-aged, bespectacled, and the mother of four grown children. When I ask my son about it, he just sighs and says wistfully, "Miss Linda has tadpoles."

I have a feeling the attraction could also have something to do with her big, flashy apron with the bunny rabbit pockets. And the way she always has fresh ground coffee beans in the sand table ready for digging and scooping and pouring and spilling. And the dozens of plastic baggies filled with homemade purple play dough. And that she sings songs with all of the correct animal sounds and finger movements. Or maybe it's because she showed him how to finger paint with ice cubes for the very first time.

Oh, sometimes I get a glimpse of how it used to be. My son will unexpectedly grab my hand and say, "Mom, will you play with me?" Then, we'll build block skyscrapers, create Lego cities, or dig moats in the sand at the park together. And for a brief time, I bask in the sunlight of being number one again.

I like to think of these moments as a sign that I won't be out of favor forever. Although a part of me wants to grab Miss Linda by the apron strings and demand my son back, another part realizes that I haven't totally lost my place on the A-list; I've just been rotated to another spot for a while. And I know when the novelty of ice painting and purple play dough wears off, I will once again reclaim my place as "The Smartest, Most Favorite Person in the Universe." At least until he starts kindergarten.

Debbie Farmer

This story was first published in *Family Fun* magazine, September 2000.

 Tethered

I'm poised on the cushioned gel seat, shins flexed, thighs taut, my feet resting on the pedals. With my back slightly hunched, arms straight and fingers coiled loosely around the foam handlebars, I begin to ride. It is early morning, and I am the only one on the trail.

After five miles the gravel path turns to smooth pavement that slides beneath my bike's tires. It continues for miles, and the jagged cliffs and steep rock walls bordering the route break up the monotony of the ride. I pedal on intuition, unaware of how I stay balanced. I am, however, very aware of the hot, steamy weather of this June morning as sweat trickles down my belly, soaking the waistband of my shorts. My T-shirt is drenched and decorated with a smattering of dead bugs.

Periodically, I change gears to accommodate the

shifts in terrain. My mind wanders as I focus on the path before me. I pedal slowly. Gradually, I increase my speed. Finally, I go all out, pedaling faster and faster until my legs can't pump any faster. Then, I lean back, let go of the handlebars, spread out my arms, and coast. For a moment, I pretend I am crossing some finish line. I imagine the tape breaking across my chest while I cruise to the applause of the cheering spectators—forgetting the reality of who I really am: the mother of a son newly diagnosed with cancer.

This is the world I want to inhabit, to be on a path of beauty instead of confronting the horrors at home. I am in charge here. I control the gears, speeding up or slowing down, changing the tension at will. Everywhere I go I carry the heaviness of guilt in my heart. I am his mom; what did I do or fail to do to make him get cancer? I pedal so I don't drink or do drugs or fall apart.

Today, I am riding in the 33,000-acre Cuyahoga Valley National Park. Today, it is my sanctuary, where I devote time to beauty. There is still beauty in the world, right?

I continue to ride for another fifteen miles. No one is in front of me or behind me. I don't feel tired. It's as if the wind is an invisible rope that pulls me along. The wildflowers tease me to get off my bike and pick them, but I continue to ride empty-handed.

I pedal into a slow glide and look up at the thin layer of clouds hanging in the sky. It is calm here, unlike my house. When you walk inside our home, you sense that something is broken. It reminds me of the oncologist's waiting room. Everyone who enters knows that Evan is ill and that we are waiting to hear the words "he's cured."

Yes, it is summer now, and the outdoors is bursting with life, but what will our lives be like in October when leaves dropped from branches are smashed flat on the bike trail?

I get off my bike and don't bother to lock it. In fact, I leave my backpack as well. I grab only my water bottle and cell phone. My heart is heavy enough.

I hike for about half a mile, straight up through ferns and prickers that sting my bare legs. I place my palms on rough rocks and rest. I see birds circling overhead. I envy their freedom. While their world soars above, mine is anchored below by grief and sorrow.

It is early Sunday morning in October. It is raining, and the thick drops blur my windshield. Streets glisten, and every branch is washed by rain. My headlights go on automatically. Thunder rolls overhead. It is windy, and I know that somewhere birds are flapping their wings aggressively, trying to depart, trying to escape, like I am.

I watch a lightning storm's distant flashes. I count—one . . . two . . . three . . . four . . . five . . . six . . . seven—as pellets of rain pound my car. I drive through it, wipers working on overdrive. The thunder finally stops, but the downpour continues. I have to slow down and slosh through it. I hate driving in the rain.

The rain sliding off my car drains into ditches along the highway. If only it were that easy to wash away my own inconsequential personal history. I feel a private excitement at this thought.

The rain keeps falling but lessens enough to let me speed up. I whiz past towns full of corralled people. People I'll never know; people who will never know me. I drive on past them, shamelessly speeding like a pro.

I grab the gear shift as if I'm grabbing someone roughly by the collar, stab the gas pedal, and start to sing: "Wild thing, da-da-da-da . . . ," accenting the *da-das* with four hard hand slaps on my leather steering wheel.

The rain finally stops, and the afternoon sun glints through my sunroof. I drive on, squinting through the tinted windshield. Though I pay but casual attention to the road, I am captive to my thoughts. It's as if they are saying, *Hey you! We're still here, inside you. You can run, but you can't hide.*

As I drive beyond my physical borders, I think

about my personal borders: who I am and why I woke up abruptly early this morning, quickly dressed, grabbed my car keys, and took off as my family slept.

I pull down the sun visor, and a sheet of paper flutters down and lands on my lap. It is Evan's latest blood-test results. I toss it angrily onto the front passenger seat. Immediately, I am transported home, to my summer and autumn from hell, to my twenty-one-year-old son, who only six months ago was diagnosed with Hodgkin's disease. His illness so encompasses our family's life that I have been stripped of my own.

A few miles earlier, my heart had lifted for a moment and I was singing in my car. Now, this—a reminder of what I've left behind. I reach for my cell phone to call home but stop. I swallow hard. A voice deep within me whispers, *Turn around.*

I pull over, get out, and stretch. I breathe in deeply through my nose, exhaling slowly through my mouth. Evan's tumor lies just beneath his clavicle, pressing on his heart and lungs. I feel a gaping hole in my center that's changed me forever. Once his umbilical chord attached us; today we are tethered by his illness.

I get back in the car and head for home.

I stop at a railroad crossing and open the windows to hear the freight train's thundering rhythm and feel its quaking vibrations. The barriers rise, and I cross the tracks.

I turn on my right turn signal and drive slowly

down my driveway toward the familiar universe waiting for me.

It is the end of December. We stand outside the
hospital doors, pausing before entering.

"I really don't want to be here," he says. "Let's go."

He knows we aren't leaving. He feels cold, yet his
palms are wet with clammy sweat; he wipes them on
his warm-up pants. Instinctively, I reach inside my front
pocket and turn off my cell phone. I bang my hip on
the doorframe as we enter the familiar chemo room.

I stretch out my tasteless gum, wrapping it around
my finger, as his nurse gently presses her fingers on
the port that is implanted just beneath the skin of
my son's chest. I look at his face and into his eyes. He
looks back at me, suffering as he flinches from her
poke. I try to distract him by insulting him.

"God, Evan, you're looking fleshy around the
middle."

Suddenly, I flash back to when he was an infant
and I used to play peek-a-boo, trying to catch him off
guard when his pediatrician gave him his baby shots.
Even then, Evan focused his eyes on his doctor's
hands, just as he is doing now.

His destiny is in her small, blue latex gloves.
All I can do is watch as she prepares the IV of
powerful drugs. The slow drips remind me of the
steady accompaniment of a ticking clock, dripping

through his veins with the regularity of a metronome. For the next five hours I watch nausea rise in him, starting at his stomach, climbing up to his throat, and flushing his face. I see the defeated expression in his eyes. It scrapes my insides raw.

For months I have felt as if I am constantly treading in deep water. Last April, when the showers made everything look new again and the foliage was just starting to bloom, his cancer had yet to be discovered. Then, it was early summer and I pedaled my bike through my guilt trips. In the fall, I drove my car for hours, wiping away tearstains from my face.

I am drowning in rage, while those outside our family's inner circle of pain float happily by in their boats of oblivion. When this is all over, I will unleash my anger. Now, I hold it all inside.

Somehow, Evan and I still manage to smile as if nothing has changed between us. In reality, through these terrible months, we have felt as though we've been blindfolded, handcuffed, and pushed into the unknown. Yet, Evan has found an inner strength, and I have found some kind of strength I never knew I had. Still, we know everything has changed. He will never just glide through life.

When radiation treatments end in six weeks, Evan will stand at the threshold of a new future. Like a sprinter pushing off hard from his starting block, he will push off and start life again, trying to feel lucky.

Finally, the IV is disconnected, and his port is flushed. Evan stands up—pale, weak-kneed, and light-headed. He has a terrible metallic taste in his mouth. Just before he walks out the door, he turns to his nurses and says, "If I'm not cured, it's your ass." His wide smile, inherited from me, fills his face.

We make our way to my car parked in the hospital's upper parking deck, just as we have twice a month for the past eight months. In a few days, it will be Christmas. Evan is finally done with chemotherapy. The air is bitterly cold, and my car is covered with a thick quilt of snow.

I turn to him. We are grinning. I high-five him, hard, almost knocking him over, as he shouts, "No more freakin' chemo!"

The snow swirls around us, and the wind makes us turn our backs to it, while I search my purse for my car keys. We tilt our heads back like our dog, Ozzie, and lick the flakes falling from the sky. Evan is still smiling.

As we get into my car, I wonder why people complain when it snows. Snow is so . . . well, benign.

As the beautiful snow falls like petals, hiding all the ugliness in the world, we drive out of the parking lot and toward home, tethered by hope and by love.

Leslie Terkel Wake

# Guess What?

"Mommy, guess what?"

"What?"

"When Mark had the ball and he wouldn't give it to me, I followed him, and guess what?"

"What?"

"I took it from him, and he said, 'good job,' but then I go'd to Nick and he took it away from me, and guess what?"

"What?" I rubbed my temples, waiting for the traffic light to turn green. My mind had drifted to the list of things to do once we got home. I heard the babble, but wasn't listening.

"I went around, and he tried to kick it away, but guess what?" he continued.

I drove the minivan away from the soccer field, lost in thought.

"Mommy, did you hear?"

"What?" I asked patiently.

"I said, I went around, and he tried to kick it away. But guess what?"

"All right, what?" I replied. My thoughts had finally been interrupted by his banter. Just then, I looked in the rearview mirror to get a glimpse of my son, Michael. He was excited about something and seemed determined to tell me—and even more determined to make me listen.

With enthusiasm, he continued telling me his story. Somewhat amused, I listened.

"I surprised him and crawled between his legs, and he didn't know I got the ball, and I kicked it to Kimmy, and she kicked it to the goal, and guess what?"

"What?" I smiled, fully engrossed in the conversation.

"And she made a goal, Mommy."

"Wow, that's awesome!"

"Yeah, it was really awesome!"

We both laughed.

I soon realized something was happening. We weren't just having a conversation. We were having a moment, the kind that comes and goes in a flash and is easily forgotten in the daily routine of life, the kind people say to cherish but is so hard to single out.

In the past, I had missed many of these moments, always too busy driving my children from Point A to

Point B, getting lunches made and meals ready, or doing other household chores. When I came home from work, I came home to my second job, the one with many hats—housekeeper, tutor, cook, storyteller. It dawned on me that my twin boys had grown from infants to six-year-olds. When did that happen?

On this brisk fall evening, Michael, normally shy and sensitive, flourished a little more as a young individual. Usually overshadowed by his brother's triumphs and his own not-so-triumphant experiences, he came alive with his own stories to tell.

Since birth, they had been together 24/7. They played together, fought together, shared the same room, and even shared classrooms in preschool and kindergarten. Everything they did, they did together. I tried to encourage individualism between my boys, but as a single parent, it was difficult. Individual time was rare. Individual time with Mom was unheard of.

In keeping with tradition, I signed them both up for soccer that fall. But halfway through the season, Michael's brother, Anthony, was on the receiving end of a rock thrown at his forehead by a classmate. The injury required stitches. Because of this turn of events, I took him out of soccer.

Sure, I thought about keeping Anthony in for the remainder of the season to teach both he and his brother the lesson of commitment and teamwork, but let's face it, Pelé he wasn't. He became totally bored with the sport. The soccer field certainly wasn't the place to try out karate moves, spin around in circles to see how long it took before he fell, or to harass and distract Michael and the other players, who truly wanted to play. So, my sister offered to take my injured child while my shy trooper and I went to the practices.

At the start of the season, the practices consisted of cold parents sitting on foldable chairs, drinking coffee or hot chocolate, and several five- and six-year-old boys and girls running haphazardly after the ball. No one remembered strategies. Their objective was to kick the ball—anywhere.

Michael always lagged behind. He seemed to be extremely self-conscious about not knowing how to play the game.

"The same kids always get to kick the ball anyway," he would say.

Not a big sports enthusiast myself, I tried to pick up bits and pieces of the game so I could practice with him. It just wasn't the same. I was Mom, not a teammate. Feeling somewhat inadequate, he longed for acceptance from his peers. He wanted to attend practices less and less, especially since his brother was no longer going.

But after a few weeks, it was obvious that this small group of players was coming together as a team. It amazed me how much they learned at that age and in such a short period of time. My little guy was no exception. Once out of his brother's shadow, he played, and he played well. His confidence returned.

That night on the drive home from practice, I noticed something different about him—a subtle difference only a parent would recognize. Yes, he was excited to play, and yes, he was getting better at it with each practice and game. But more important, he belonged. He was a part of something—not as a brother, not as a twin, but as himself. And he wanted badly to share that with me.

He was on cloud nine that evening, and we bonded in a special way. With no one to distract or stifle his glory and with no self-esteem issues dampening his excitement, he was proud of his performance, and so was I.

He'd played very well that practice, and on the ride home he was a chatterbox. Tired, cold, distracted by life's usual never-ending to-dos and slightly irritated at his babble, I'd only half listened . . . until it hit me: This is one of those cherished, and fleeting, moments. And guess what? I grabbed hold of it and savored it. I stopped and listened and applauded and rejoiced. And guess what? It was good, very good.

Carmen Rosado

Courtside

"A guy I grew up with got hit by a truck in London because he looked the wrong way before he crossed the street," I told my twenty-year-old son the evening before he left to travel through Europe. "So, remember," I said as he threw a basketball into the hoop attached to our garage, "You need to look right first, not left, when they drive on the opposite side of the street."

"I'm not going to England," he reminded me, dribbling the ball low and fast.

"Still," I explained, "It's an example of a cross-cultural danger. It's a metaphor: Things can come at you from the other direction, and I want you to be prepared. That guy is dead."

Lev tossed the ball against the backboard and jumped to tip it into the basket. "How embarrassing," he said.

This talk is not going well, I thought. I sat on the wooden steps of my back porch, untied and retied my running shoes as I tried to decide what I really wanted to say. I am not, to tell the truth, the least bit concerned about my son crossing the street safely; he's the one who stopped me from getting on the wrong side of a moving sidewalk when we arrived at Heathrow Airport three years ago. "Stay to your left here," he'd said, grabbing my arm and saving me from heading face-first into a pile of gliding Englishmen.

Like most parents of young adults, I'm more worried about things that are not as easy to speak about as the flow of traffic. I'm afraid he'll use illegal drugs and get locked up in a Spanish jail. I'm scared he'll ride a motorcycle without wearing a helmet and crack his skull open. I'm terrified he'll have unprotected sex and get AIDS.

What's more, I'm still convinced, despite all evidence to the contrary, that if I were nearby I could keep him safe. Never mind that in my presence he's swum out too far, jumped from too high up, broken bones, and caught viruses. Never mind that, when he was seven, I was the one who threw the baseball that hit him in the jaw. Still, I insist on believing that I can prevent him from getting hurt.

It's because I'm the mother, I thought, as I rested my elbows on my knees and studied the crack on the bottom step. Doesn't that mean I have the power to protect?

When I looked up, Lev was standing in front of me, spinning the ball on one finger. In his hands a basketball looks as if it's magnetic—it sticks to his palm, rolls up his arm, returns to him from any surface.

"I want you to promise me you'll be careful about drugs, sex, and rock 'n' roll," I said, trying not to sound too heavy-handed, trying, actually, to be as graceful with him as he is with a basketball.

"I'll give up rock 'n' roll all summer," Lev said, smiling and tossing the ball lightly into my open hands.

Maybe I should have stopped there. He understood I was scared, and I understood that anything else I might say would probably be information he already knew.

But I couldn't risk it; I had to be certain. What I presume my son knows is very often wrong now. He certainly knows how to pay attention and think quickly, and how to hop on a moving sidewalk in the right direction, but I don't believe he knows about the fragility of life. I don't believe he's supposed to know that yet.

I didn't, at his age. I drove a car with no seatbelts and a bicycle with no brakes, and when those weren't available, I hitchhiked to class. I walked alone in the dark to show that women could take back the night, and I swallowed a tab of something bitter, believing a friend who said it would help me write poetry.

I think it's important, at my son's stage of life, to imagine that anything is possible—to put on a backpack and travel the world. And I think it's important, at my stage of life, to let go of the illusion that I can protect him. But I can still teach caution. I can still say: *Be careful. Please, dear child, be very, very careful.*

So that evening, I told my son about Spanish jails, even though I know absolutely nothing about Spanish jails. I reminded him that just because there are no helmet laws in a country doesn't mean there are no motorcycle accidents there. And I spoke, one more time, about sexually transmitted diseases.

Then, the ball in his court, I pulled on my sweater, leaned back on the railing, and watched him play.

Wendy Lichtman

This story was previously published as "Mothering After the Kid Is Gone" in the *San Francisco Chronicle*, September 15, 1999, and as "Growing Pains" in *Working Mother*, June 2001.

Mom and Gentle Bear

Gentle Bear came out of my womb in the ninety-fifth percentile of height and weight for babies. In fact, he didn't come willingly or on time; he waited to be drawn out through a gash in my abdomen. They whisked him away to neonatal intensive care, and it was twelve hours before I saw him.

The well-intentioned pediatrician visited my bedside and announced, "I don't know if we have a little boy or girl, because I can't feel any testicles."

My child had all the other equipment required for a male child. I read that these things could happen. I cried, because I didn't know how I'd retrieve the birth announcements from the mail.

An experienced neonatal nurse reassured me, "I don't know what that doctor's talking about. I can feel two. They're high, but they're here."

We took our big baby boy home.

Gentle Bear was our first child, and I was a keener. I read the parenting books. I attended all of the available workshops. At one workshop, in particular, the facilitator asked all those present to call out what they wanted their children to be like when they left home. "Independent." "Loving." "Educated." "Clean." "Snappy dresser." "Devoted." The list was impressive.

Upon reflection I called out, "It looks like we're expecting 'Second Coming' to walk out of our doors."

When everything about your child is large, it's hard to explain that it takes longer to coordinate muscles and limbs to pass the expected milestones.

"No, Mom, he's not rolling over yet, but he sleeps through the night."

"No, Mom, he's not sitting by himself yet, but he loves his Jolly Jumper."

"Why does his tongue stick out like that? Are you sure he's not mentally challenged? Have you had him tested?"

"He's fine."

"Sorry I can't come in to work today; Gentle Bear is in the hospital. No, I don't know when he'll be out. Yes, I realize I missed work last month because he was sick."

"What is it, doctor, he seems to be sick so often?"

"G. B. isn't large due to genetics; he's large due to an abnormality of genetics."

"What does that mean?"

"We don't know; there hasn't been much research done into this syndrome."

"Look, honey, Santa brought you a big-wheeled bike just like the one you rode in the hospital."

"Don't cry, Gentle Bear. It's okay; everyone spills once in a while."

"But, Mommy, I don't want to spill. I'm big."

"Oh, sweetie, you're big, but you're little, too."

"Look at this kid's biceps. He's got quite the arms on him."

"Gentle Bear, be careful when you grab something from Jay Jaye; you don't want to hurt him."

"Look at this kid's feet; they're huge."

"Be careful, Gentle Bear, when you run into Bobbie; you're so much bigger than he is."

"Hey, kid, don't hide behind your mommy. What grade are you in, big buddy?"

"He's not in school. He's not old enough."

"Whoa! You sure are one big fella. What's your mama feed you?"

"Gentle Bear, if someone wants to go ahead of you, let him. Okay? It's only one spot."

"But, Mom, Aaron teases me. One day I'm going to plow him."

"Yes, I know, but maybe he had a bad day. Just walk away."

"Mom can you make a G.I. Joe pants and shirt like

mine for my Cabbage Patch?"

"Sure thing."

"But, Mom, I want to play hockey. I'll be careful."

"I know you would, Gentle Bear, but some of those bigger kids think you're older than you are, and they might hurt you."

"Would you like to come ice-fishing with your old grandpa over the holidays?"

"Yippee! Grandpa, can I put the wood in the stove?"

"Gentle Bear, you have a little brother."

"I'll take good care of him, Mom."

"Be careful how you hold him. Be careful when you pull him, Gentle Bear."

"G. B. expresses his ideas clearly in class discussions. He has written some interesting stories."

"You're a great swimmer, Gentle Bear. You've got power in your strokes."

"Hey, watch the giant trip over his feet."

"Mom, I was almost last in the race again."

"I know, Gentle Bear, but you can build Legos better than anyone I know."

"Yah. Without the instructions, too."

"G. B. works very hard at school. In his position as hall monitor, he treats the younger children with respect."

"Gentle Bear, do you want to go snowmobiling in the mountains with Dad and his friends?"

"Whoopee!"

"Gentle Bear, would you help me move this table?"

"Sure, Mom."

"Mom, Jason really teases me on the bus. I don't think I can take it much longer."

"Okay, Gentle Bear, tomorrow when he gets off the bus, you have my permission—clobber him."

"So, how'd it go?"

"Nah, I didn't have to clobber him. I just said I would and that was enough. Thanks, Mom."

"You're welcome."

"I sure wish our school had a football team. I'd be great."

"Yes, you would."

"Mom, I'm going to join Navy Cadets."

"That's a great idea; you're so comfortable swimming and driving a boat."

"And tying knots."

"Well, G. B., I can say you've finally grown into your body. "

"Thanks, Doc. I'm kind of used to being the biggest in the class."

"Mom, I'm not sure I want to go to university. I like to work with my hands."

"I know, Gentle Bear, but Dad would like you to try."

"Mom, I'm joining the Navy Reserves on weekends and holidays. I really need the adventures."

"Great idea; it beats mowing lawns."

"Mom, university isn't for me."

"Where did this come from?"

"I've been thinking about it for a long time."

"But you're doing well in your classes."

"I know, but I want to work with my hands, too."

"You'll finish this semester?"

"Sure. Mom, how are your classes going?"

"I was just thinking about the question my philosophy professor asked the class today: 'What are we prepared to die for?'"

"That's easy—my country."

"Really, Gentle Bear? Most of the class came up with our family and friends."

"Mom, I'm going to enlist in the Navy."

"What exactly does that mean?"

"I go away for eight weeks of basic training."

Week Seven: test week. "Drill, no problem; I am basically a drill god."

"Congratulations, Son. You're so handsome in your uniform."

"Mom, I'm going to be stationed in British Columbia."

"So far away."

"Mom, I'm in the Navy. We need water, and we're a little short of that here on the prairie."

"We'll come out to visit. We'll tour your boat."

"*Frigate*, Mom."

"It rains out there a lot."

"I know; I'll miss snowmobiling and ice fishing."

"But your boat is bigger . . . I know, *ship.*"

"I'm an Able Seaman. They're sending us to the Persian Gulf."

"Be careful, Gentle Bear. I love you."

"Will do. Love you, too, Mom."

Times Colonist, Monday, September 25, 2000: "While in the Gulf, HMCS *Calgary* has been part of a three-ship task group enforcing United Nations Security Council resolutions and sanctions against Iraq, inspecting vessels coming and going from Iraq and allowing only humanitarian and nonmilitary vessels to pass."

"I filled out the paperwork for my Peace Keeping medal."

"I'm so proud, Son."

"I'll be home in time to decorate the tree."

"I'll be here, Gentle Bear. I'll be here."

Annette M. Bower

 Heavensent

Not long ago, on a beautiful spring afternoon in Arizona, I attended the wedding of my high school friend Mike. While the guests arrived and were being seated, I sat quietly near the front row, admiring the elegantly decorated altar and enjoying the lush landscape and lakeside view. The breeze was cool but pleasant, the sky slightly overcast but with no prediction of rain. As I waited for the ceremony to begin, I glanced over the program and my eyes fell on "A Mother's Blessing." A lump came to my throat, as I was reminded that Mike's mother had passed away unexpectedly several years before. I assumed the blessing would be a passage or prayer, delivered by the bride's mother.

The music started, and the procession began. The ceremony unfolded brilliantly, exactly as it was outlined in the program. Just before it was time for

Mike and Julie to exchange their vows as husband and wife, Julie's mother stood up from her seat in the front row and gracefully walked to the altar. At that precise moment, I noticed some faint sprinkles of rain on my arm. I looked around, but no other guests seemed to notice them.

Julie's mother spoke about the joy of being a mother and how important a child's wedding day is for any mother. Again, I fought back tears as I thought of my own five-month-old son at home and how much I'd want to be there for his wedding. She asked Mike for permission to speak on behalf of his late mother in giving the blessing. He nodded a teary-eyed yes as a light sprinkle began to fall from the sky. Now, I saw that the other guests were noticing the light rain-drops, too. I was relieved, for the bride's sake, that the rain wasn't enough to threaten the ceremony. Julie's mother proceeded to tell of the power of a mother's love. She spoke of how proud both mothers were of their children on this momentous day. Somehow, she kept her composure as she read a beautiful passage from a book.

I wasn't doing so well in the composure depart-ment. Mike was an only child, and he had been really close to his mother. It pained me to imagine how much he missed her on that day, at that moment. By then, the drizzle was felt by all. Then, an over-whelming feeling came over me, a presence. Glancing around, I knew others felt it, too. I looked up at the grayish blue clouds, haloed by the sunlight illuminating them from behind. I thought of heaven and how close it suddenly felt. I thought of a mother who couldn't be there on her son's glorious wedding day. Or could she?

The mother's blessing came to a close, and then Julie's mother said something obviously impromptu. She smiled compassionately at Mike, who was now wiping away the tears with one hand while holding his bride's hand tightly in the other. She told him she knew his mother was watching from above, because we could all feel her teardrops falling from heaven. She had said exactly what every guest, including myself, had been thinking.

A chill ran through me as I realized that what I was feeling was not my imagination or a coincidence. Mike's mother was there for her only son's wedding day, and we all sensed her presence.

In reverent silence, Julie's mother returned to her seat, and the minister pronounced the happy couple man and wife. As the bride and groom kissed and walked arm in arm down the petal-strewn path, the gentle raindrops suddenly faded away. For the rest of the day, not a single raindrop fell.

Sarah L. Hess

Naming Names

When my younger son, Aaron, was three or so, he had serious ambitions: He wanted to be a racecar driver or a superhero when he grew up. At about that time, I gave him the chance to name a litter of kittens. They were, perhaps, the only felines ever to answer to the unforgettable (no matter how hard I tried) names of "Bionic Man," "Bionic Woman," "Bionic Man Junior," and "Bionic Woman Junior."

A year or two later, when he suggested the name "G.I. Joe" for a certain bundle of Creamsicle fluff, I exercised a mother's veto and named the kitten "Katie," instead. As Aaron grew older, I managed to restrain myself from inviting him to name the various puppies, kittens, fish, and ferrets joining our household. I just couldn't picture myself calling the dog in with a name based on a computer game: "Queen of

Doom! Queen of Doom! Come in, girl!" Nor was I crazy for the names "Beavis" and "Duke Nukem."

As time went by, the life of a racecar driver or a superhero appealed less to Aaron. He became much more practical and mature about the various career paths beckoning to him: jobs such as disc jockey ("They actually pay you to play music all day!"), rock star, and pro football player. His future profession was sure to be exciting, extremely lucrative, and—most important of all—something that would make him famous.

But, as we all know, life sometimes has a way of interfering with our most glamorous aspirations. And so, my son eventually went into the service. He and his wife, Wendy, were stationed in Germany. When we asked, speaking rapidly at eighty-plus cents a minute, how he liked his job, he laughed and said, "Guys! I throw huge bags of mail all day. How do you think I like it?"

Soon after their daughter was born, we flew over on the wings of our desire to hold our first grandchild. On the way, I wondered out loud, "Can any baby in the world possibly live up to the elegance of the name 'Victoria Grace'?"

It took me about two seconds to discover the answer to that question. Victoria was that rare combination, in my absolutely unbiased opinion, of brilliant and beautiful—even at the tender age of three months.

I wasn't surprised to find myself falling totally, help-lessly in love with her. But what I was unprepared for, absolutely, was the experience of watching my son with his daughter.

As soon as I saw Aaron at the airport, I detected something different about him. His eyes sparkled as he held his daughter up to meet her grandparents.

"She smiles and coos and laughs," he told us proudly. "And don't you think she's as beautiful as her mother?"

Indeed we did, we told him, curving our arms around Victoria, inhaling sweet baby fragrance, and beaming at Wendy.

"She likes to be held like this," he told us, demonstrating.

In short order we learned about Victoria's sleeping habits, eating habits, and burping habits. We were given the tour of the new parents' apartment: Victoria's beautifully decorated bedroom, her favorite toys, The Swing, and the nonessentials, like the bathroom, kitchen, and our bed.

We spent the week passing around Victoria with great pleasure, each of the four of us claiming turns to hold her. When we ate, she charmed us from The Swing, that battery-operated wonder next to the dining table. One evening we went out to dinner. Victoria began to fuss. This was unusual. Victoria wasn't much of a fusser.

"She's bored," my son told us. "I'll swing her in her infant seat. She loves that; it reminds her of The Swing at home. There's not enough room in here, so I'll go outside."

Every so often, one of us would leave the chow mein and step out into the clear German air to check on them. There he'd be, his arm swinging pendulum-style, back and forth, Victoria in her infant seat dangling from his hand, content . . . as long as he kept on ticking.

"Isn't your arm getting tired?" I asked him.

He shrugged. "I throw mail all day; this is nothing."

No pro football player, I thought, *ever gets a workout like this one.*

In the car on the way home, music was selected carefully. "Victoria loves U2," the disc jockey explained. Then he drove, on the no-speed-limit autobahn, like a racecar driver.

"If you drive too slowly, you can get rear-ended," Wendy told us, no doubt noticing our white knuckles.

Having survived the ride home, I watched my granddaughter peeled like a banana by her dad and then expertly pj-ed. I can tell you, no rock star has ever had a more adoring audience than Victoria listening to Dad coo to her. Why, to see the look in her eyes, you'd swear she was gazing up at a superhero—or at least someone extremely famous.

One of these days, I've got something to tell my

son: Aaron, you've grown up to be something a lot more important than a racecar driver, a disc jockey, a rock star, a pro football player, or even a superhero.

But then, I don't think he needs to be told. I have a hunch he already knows.

There's one more thing I want to add: Aaron, I am so very, very grateful Wendy helped you out with choosing that baby's name.

Terry Miller Shannon

This story was first published as "All He Wanted to Be" in the *Christian Science Monitor*, August 25, 1997.

The Writing on the Wall

I know the boy wasn't born in a barn. I know because I was there, and I distinctly remember giving birth in a hospital. But just look at this bedroom! Dirty clothes and candy wrappers lie crumpled on the floor. A can of pop sits open on the desk right beside the homework assignment that I'm pretty sure was due yesterday. And a half-eaten peanut butter sandwich peeks out from under the bed. It's a wonder the basement's not crawling with ants. Of course, if it were, maybe I could train the critters to do the kid's laundry and carry his dishes back upstairs.

I hear the phone ring in the hall, but I ignore it. It's probably just the haz-mat team. Maybe someone's tipped them off to my son's private little dump site. I can see it now. Guys in rubber suits and gas masks storm in and stop dead in their tracks. I imagine the alarm on their faces as they back out again.

I look over at the far wall of the room. I know the kid likes to draw, but does he have to doodle on the plaster? Yes, he does, because he's Kevin—my "don't worry, be happy" guy. He's always telling me the mess and confusion in here is no big deal. But I do worry, and it doesn't make me happy, and I do think it's a big deal. Doodles on the wall? I can see the writing on it. I imagine him five years from now: twenty-one, too disorganized for college, and too sloppy to land a decent job.

I don't care how tired he is after snowboarding today, the second he gets home he's going to have to dig this place out. And touch up the paint. Do his laundry. Disinfect.

"Mom! Phone!" my younger son hollers down the stairs to me. "Some guy from the ski lodge."

Kevin's flipped on his snowboard and cracked open his head. He's unconscious. The hospital in the little city at the base of the mountain is sixty miles from home. All the way there, I wonder why cars can't fly. What good is modern technology if it still takes an hour to get to the emergency room?

I park in the hospital lot and run across the pavement. The doctor is waiting for me just inside the double doors of the building. He tells me that Kevin is awake, alert, and probably going to be fine. I can take him home in a couple of hours. After we are home, I'm to watch Kevin carefully. I'm to note any changes in behavior or attitude that might signal the need for additional medical attention.

I bundle Kevin into the car and begin watching him in the rearview mirror. All the way home.

"Mom, I'm fine. It's no big deal," Kevin says to my reflection.

"Mom, you can't follow me into the shower," he tells me the next morning.

"Mom, if you keep staring at me, I am going to go crazy," Kevin repeats for the forty-ninth time, a couple of hours later. He's sitting on his bed. I've cleared a path over and settled on the desk chair.

Of course, he's right. I can't note strange behavior if I'm the one who's causing it. What we need is a project.

"We could clean your room," I say, gesturing around the pit.

"Hey, I've got a serious head injury here," Kevin says and grins.

"We could paint the walls."

"Cool! Let's do a mural."

I was thinking more along the lines of a nice, solid, creamy white, but . . . "Okay," I agree. Kevin decides we should paint something to commemorate the accident. He suggests a crazy portrait of me, because that's how I've been acting. Very funny.

"I know: First, we'll make the wall look cracked," Kevin says and laughs at my confused look. "Get it? Like my head."

He gets down on his knees and reaches under the bead. He pulls out a box and opens the lid. Inside the box are his art supplies. Everything is neat and tidy. Markers are in their package. Pencils are sharpened. Paint brushes are clean. I'm surprised. How'd the supplies escape the havoc all around them?

Kevin chooses markers, a couple of tubes of paint, and a brush. He sketches out a design and then goes to work. Under his hand the bedroom plaster begins to look as if it's peeling away and exposing a brick wall. I am amazed.

"When did you get so talented?" I ask.

"It's no big deal," Kevin says. "I just think about how stuff should look and then try to draw it."

He begins sketching again on the wall. I'm given the job of assistant to the artist. I clean brushes, cap markers, and sharpen pencils. While we work, we talk. Kevin mentions, casually, that he's been thinking about going to art school after graduation.

Graduation? College? My heart stumbles. Last time I checked, the kid wasn't even taking high school seriously. I look over at the late assignment still sitting on the desk. Kevin glances over his shoulder, following my gaze.

"Don't worry. I've got it under control. Ms. Shannon gave me an extension on the due date."

He turns and continues working. The wall now looks like the side of an old tumble-down building.

A sign on the side of the building reads, "Flip's Snowboard Shop." A crazy-looking lady stands under the sign, staring into the room. She holds an oversize sheet of paper marked with an Rx in the corner. I can't help myself. I grab a marker and write "Clean Room" on the prescription sheet.

Kevin laughs. "I figured you'd put 'homework' first," he says.

"You told me you had it under control," I tell him.

"Well, I've got to finish high school to get on with the fun stuff."

We step back to admire our work. Kevin throws an arm across my shoulder. I've got to admit the wall looks great, and I appreciate the jokes in the painting. The faux cracked plaster for Kevin's cracked head. "Flip" and his snowboard shop. And me, the crazy lady, with my prescription for life.

But it's not just the mural that amazes me. It's the writing on the wall. My "don't worry, be happy" kid is learning to happily worry a little over what's a big deal to him. And I need to step back and let it happen. I imagine ahead five years. Life, as I'd want him to love it, is just beginning.

Then he'll have to train his own bugs to do the laundry.

Judy L. Forney

All Aboard

I first saw Jesse from the window of a trolley in Philadelphia. Straggling behind his father, small and fireplug-shaped in his brown toggle-coat, he was scuffing the toes of his orthopedic oxfords on the sidewalk. Beneath a Prince Valiant haircut, his small features were contorted in a scowl. I sighed, pulled the bell cord, and got off.

"She's not staying overnight," Jesse announced, his lower lip turned down so much it made his chin look pruney. His hazel eyes were narrowed and his brows were knit so tightly they met above his nose. A yellow bubble of mucus puffed in and out of one nostril.

I waited for Marty's answer. My friends had warned me not to get involved with men who already had children, but he and I were just friends. A female medical student had a lot to prove in 1973, and romantic entanglements could squander precious time. Besides, Marty wasn't my type. I had come merely to collect on the homemade-from-a-jar spaghetti dinner he'd promised me.

"Don't worry," Marty reassured his son. "She's not staying over tonight."

Fifteen minutes later, while the pasta boiled, I munched a leaf of iceberg lettuce and said, "This may be crazy, but I'm not sure you should let him run your love life. That kind of power isn't good for a three-year-old."

Marty looked up from his efforts to open the jar of Ragu sauce. "You mean you'd stay?" The lid popped. "If he wasn't here, I mean; if he was at his mother's."

I laughed and wandered into Marty's room, where Jesse was lying on the bed—a double mattress on the floor—and running a small metal car back and forth on the wood floor.

"Hey, Jess."

"Go away."

The same snot was still percolating, but faster now. He looked about to cry and, if he did, the evening would be ruined. I pulled a piece of paper from a pad, grabbed a pencil, and dropped down next to him.

"Do you like trains?" I tried to use the tone of the jolly, inclusive adults on *Sesame Street*.

He sniffled, a lonely, desperate sound.

With equal desperation, my pencil flew across the paper, drawing an engine, the old-fashioned kind with a tall smokestack, a bell, and a window with a smiling face peering out from under a striped cap labeled "Jesse the Engineer."

"That's my name," he said, now kneeling next to me, one dirty little hand on my shoulder.

I held my breath, just as I would if a wild bird had landed to eat out of my palm, and I added a coal car.

"Box car," he commanded.

A nice one appeared on the page, with a door bearing a big X made by sturdy wood planks.

"Caboose."

The caboose had another striped-hat figure waving a lantern.

"Jesse," he said, stabbing the page with one stout finger.

Two Jesses on one page were A-okay in his world. As soon as his name was added, he pulled the page away, got up, and got a new piece of paper.

"Again."

"Say 'please.'"

He stared at me, our eyes level now that he was standing. A shadow of doubt or anger crossed his face, and then lifted. "Please."

Within two months he was calling me "Mommy," and I was sleeping with his father in my little three-room house downtown. When Jesse stayed over, he slept between us. I said nothing in the night when a chubby arm reached past my head to post boogers on the bedroom wall. Mornings, his father slept in while we walked to the local Greek diner, where Jesse's favorite drink was on tap. "Pancakes and Hawai-nan Punch," he'd order, throwing a tight victory fist into the air. I'd sit across from him, nursing a cup of strong coffee, trying to deny that I was falling for a man, in part, because he was part owner of the love of my life.

Jesse lived most days with his mother in an apartment whose door was kicked in one day by her violent boyfriend. When I asked Jesse about Willie, his face closed up like that Hawai-nan Punch fist, but with a lot less bravado.

We often visited old neighbors of Marty's in Jesse's building. One time I went to buy bread for dinner, accompanied by the husband of that couple. On the way out of the building, we ran into Jesse and his mother. Jesse's eyes lit up when he saw me; he ran and grabbed my legs and said, "Don't let her take me, Mommy!"

His mother's face grew spaghetti-sauce red; she pulled him away. I held off crying until I was in the car.

A week later, Marty had me accompany him to the divorce counselor he was seeing.

"I don't think you should see Jesse anymore. It's

confusing him," said the counselor, a large woman twenty years our senior. Cheerful prints by Marty's ex-wife adorned her walls.

"How the hell can you say that?" I raged as calmly as I could. "A kid doesn't call another woman 'Mommy' unless his relationship with his mother is really weird."

Later in the car, Marty said, "She's the expert. She'll help his mother fight for sole custody if I don't do what she says."

He had already spent a month's salary talking to lawyers, only to have them say, "Forget it. You don't stand a chance." Men didn't win child custody battles in the early seventies. Not in Pennsylvania. A man Marty knew had been denied custody even after his ex-wife abandoned their children at an orphanage in the middle of the state to run off to be a hooker in New York. That story and others had burned Marty's usual scrappiness out of him.

"You can't spend time with him right now," he said.

I was banished from Jesse's life for months. When next I saw him, he was distant, shy, and seething with anger. He remained that way while I mourned, unable to explain the situation in four-year-old terms.

I continued to do most of the thankless work of mothering: taking him to the emergency room when we picked him up to find he had another ear infection and had been burning with fever for days, buying him new shoes on my one free weekend each month, making sure his homework got done. His mother made birthday parties and Halloween costumes. I felt like a no-fun also-ran. Besides, I missed him, even after his sister was born. My love for her was different than my love for him. Jesse and I had chosen to be friends; we'd chosen to be family.

We moved to Colorado when Jesse was eleven, sure we were leaving him behind except for summer visits. His sister was only six and always carsick, so she flew with me to Denver while Jesse drove with his father.

"I don't want to go back," he said to us one day, sliding a piece of broccoli under his mashed potatoes.

On parental autopilot, I reached over and pulled it back out to the center of his plate.

"Besides, the schools are on strike in Philadelphia." It seemed he'd been following the news.

My husband didn't say a word.

"You'll have to talk it over with your mother," I said. "We can't without her consent; you know that."

Jesse called her that night and raced into our bedroom, leaping on the bed, his eyes gleaming, his fist raised in triumph. "I can stay. She just wants to come out and see if it's nice here."

"That's wonderful," we said, sharing a hug.

The telephone rang. "Send him back, you bastard,"

his mother screamed, her voice ringing in my ears, though I stood ten feet away.

Marty started for the living room, where Jesse was watching TV. I jumped up, my heartbeat thumping like the rumble of a steam engine in my ears. "You do her dirty work for her, and I'll leave you! He'll think you don't want him if you say he has to go back. You're not doing that to him."

I stepped ahead of him and went to the couch.

"Jesse, I want you to be aware that your mother might come take you."

His jaw jutted. "My mommy wouldn't do that to me."

Shamed and uncertain, I didn't add the second sentence I'd planned: "But we'll come for you no matter what."

Susan got a court order in Philadelphia by lying, saying Jesse was being held against his will. Without warning, she brought two policemen to his junior high school to enforce the order. When Jesse saw them, he tried to run but was outmaneuvered by the horrified cops, who tied him to a chair when he kicked and bit them. The policemen, risking contempt charges, refused to remove him until his father got a chance to say goodbye.

In Philadelphia Family Court, Jesse was asked if he wanted to live with his father because our resort town was serene and safe.

He replied, "I'd want to be with my dad if he'd moved to Cleveland."

The custody suit put us $15,000 in debt; it was the best investment we ever made. Jesse came home to be ours. Or at least, Marty's—he remained aloof with me.

At fourteen, Jesse took his father aside and said simply, "I won't go back."

His mother didn't bother to come visit and didn't demand holidays and summers, so he didn't go to her. He never referred to her as "Mom" again. That was now my title, though seemingly mere window dressing for his friends; our small town was still a haven of the nuclear family.

Guilt-ridden at having "won," I went on a campaign to heal the break between Jesse and his mother. Just before he turned eighteen, he was finally convinced to call her for the first time in years.

Afterward he said to me, "I was right, and you were wrong. I'm not talking to her again."

"Jesse," I said, "the more people who love you, the better off you are."

His newly deorthodontured smile shone. "I know you think that, Mom. I didn't always know it, though. I felt angry for years, like you abandoned me when I needed you. I don't know why I felt that way." He shrugged. "But now, that feeling's gone." He turned as if to go, then stopped. "Oh, I've decided what I want for my birthday."

Two weeks later, the whole family was in the private judges' chambers of the 14th Judicial District of the State of Colorado, the warm and comfortable private chambers of my friend Becky Love Kourlis.

"Thank you," Judge Love was saying, wiping her eyes. "That was the nicest thing I've ever presided over."

I'd just adopted my son. Jesse had checked with the county and found that, at eighteen, he could be adopted without having his birth mother give up her rights.

"I want you to be my real, authentic mom," he said. "You asked me what I wanted for my birthday; that's it."

Marty had been Jesse's father for the entire eighteen years of his life. And there had never been a time when Jesse and his sister weren't related by blood. But I had only been his mother from the time he was eleven. I'd never felt legitimate or even morally correct being called "Mom," even as I worked to help pay for the house he lived in, made his school lunches, kept his sometimes obnoxious little sister away while I helped him with algebra, and kissed him good night.

After the adoption, we went out for ice cream—all of us, the whole authentic family.

Judith Beck

 # Brave Hearts

He went because I expected him to. A little brown-eyed, brown-haired boy who had been just fine at home, thank you.

But because I asked it of him, he walked into the classroom with only one tentative backward look and a faint tremor of lip. He wore a yellow shirt and carried something in his hand. I do not now remember what it was. A packet of supplies, maybe. A new pencil, perhaps. It didn't matter. We had bought it to make him feel ready for school, whether he was or not. Armor purchased in school supplies—a tablet to make you brave, a pencil to make you belong, a red crayon for courage.

So he held it tightly, this bit of school armor. And only looked back once. But I knew, and he knew, that it was the bravest thing he had ever done. You can tell a lot about a kid by looking at his back. How the spine goes suddenly stiff and the shoulders get all scarecrowish.

How the little body suddenly looks unprotected in a yellow knit shirt. The feet that had run so confidently the summer day before now drag a little on the school's industrial-strength carpet.

Because he was No. 2 Kid, he was born portable. He learned to hang out early, cadging pennies for the office gum machine, sitting with a comic book while I rewrote one more paragraph. Putting off, laying back, taking it easy, waiting to go to the next place, the grocery store, the cleaners, the city hall, the garage, the doctor's office, the fabric store. I lost him there once, in the fabric store, and found him in the satins, his thumb and forefinger instinctively kneading the same silkiness that trimmed his favorite blanket. His other thumb in his mouth. Just waiting.

His sister would have shoved the satin aside and screamed. She had things to do. She would have panicked. Not No. 2 Kid. He seized the moment and the satin and kicked back, patiently waiting for what came next.

After five years of being led around and liking it, on this day he was on his own, walking into the strange building with the echoing halls, a room full of kids, and a college-taught smile that said out loud, "Welcome to kindergarten." And then the hidden message: *Welcome to the big time, kid.* He had this yellow tag around his neck, as though UPS planned to ship him somewhere far away.

We were all very brave—he and his father and I—that morning. His much-schooled sister kept slapping him between his bony shoulder blades, saying now he would go to school just like she did. He looked back at this blue-eyed paragon/sibling with his deep-brown eyes clearly indicating he had no interest in being like her.

I heard not long ago of a mother who could not convince her child to stay peacefully behind in kindergarten. I heard that just for a moment there, she almost relented. You could see her, a witness said, thinking, *What the heck, I'll just scoop him up and take him to work with me, and we'll forget about this silly business of school and work and play and responsibility. We'll just chuck it all.* Then her back got all scarecrowish, and she bent to the hard labor of shoving her child from the nest into the world/classroom.

I've also heard of mothers whose kids ran from them, hell-bent for education and professional advancement. But even moms of overachievers stand in the door with their lips in tremor.

Walking in there was the bravest thing No. 2 Kid ever did. So, I had to be brave, too. I imprinted the memory of that frail back sheathed in cotton. I saw his brown eyes wishing he could stay with me. I sent him the same message with my own eyes, and then I turned and fled to have my cry on the steering wheel.

Sharon Nesbit

What Goes Around

I am becoming Mrs. Sarti, the bee-hived Amazon who towered her power over me and the rest of the seventh-grade girls who gaga-ed over her youngest son, Mark. It all began after morning prayers for peace and midwinter announcements about First Friday confessions. Sister Patricia knocked once on our door, proclaiming in her blessings-from-Heaven pitch that we were to have a new student, a new male student, at St. Matthew's Elementary. He was a transfer from public school. We were to show him how Catholics behave. Welcome him into our close-knit fold.

"Yes, Sister," we chorused, shifting in our plaid pleated skirts, anxious and hopeful as we watched mother and son follow the black-and-white nun through our gray classroom door.

The boy blushed and let out a grin. His mother matched it with a grimace and a bat of her heavily made-up eyes. I winced at her too-tight skirt, spray-slick hair, and rounds of unblended rouge on her sallow cheeks. He must take after his father, I concluded, turning my attention full force on the boy.

Sister Patricia said his name and pointed him toward the third row. Mrs. Sarti silently stared at us before being dismissed by the nun. I watched both women walk out the door and listened to the *click-clack* of high heels and the brush of beads move quickly out of range.

Mark Sarti was not so hurried. He shuffled to the spare seat behind Philip Rhodes. I watched as the new boy folded his legs beneath the chair and folded his hands, saintlike, on the top of the desk. I turned to see the other girls watching him, too. We nodded our approval through raised brows and lips, our genuflect to God for finally sending us a savior.

It wasn't that Mark Sarti was wonderful. He was simply different. He was new. We'd seen the other boys since first grade, witnessed their good deeds and bad habits, and frankly, we were bored with life as we knew it at age thirteen.

Then, behold Mark Sarti. He was taller than the rest, and his hair was longer than the regulation butch. He had a sly smile and a cute wink. He knew right away to laugh at Mr. Kraker's stupid jokes and to roll his eyes at Mrs. Campbell's outlandish wardrobe.

Being a bit overweight and a bit under-height, I

used my chatterbox approach as the self-appointed Welcome Wagon for the St. Matthew's seventh grade. As such, I was the first to officially introduce myself to the new boy. I don't remember what I said, but I do recall that I made a vow, right then and there, that Mark Sarti would be the very first boy I would kiss. And he was. It happened weeks later at the school skating party, when a backward all-skate sidelined me to the dark side of the rink, near arcade games and kids who couldn't stand on wheels.

But that's really about as far as my memory goes with Mark Sarti. He went on to kiss other girls and to break other hearts. I've heard he's been married twice and has at least three tall boys of his own. That means that Mrs. Sarti is a grandmother. Heaven help the girls.

Because it is Mrs. Sarti, not her son, who I muse about most when my thoughts return to seventh grade. I see Mrs. Sarti giving dirty looks across the gymnasium bleachers as the chorus of "Go Mark" sails down the basketball court. I hear Mrs. Sarti clicking her tongue as she looks at our rolled up uniform skirts and platform shoes. I wince as Mrs. Sarti slaps down the phone receiver after our giggled requests about Mark's presence at home on a Saturday night.

It was Mrs. Sarti who pulled her son's hand away from our hold. And it was Mrs. Sarti who watched behind her mirrored sunglasses as we dunked and splashed, girls chasing boys, that summer at the Brownley pool.

How we hated Mrs. Sarti. But how her son adored her. He called her "Rose," her real first name, as he playfully slugged her in the arm or gave her a sideways glance to her silent warning to "be careful of the girls."

Oh, that Rose, she was prickly. She never sweetened toward us. She pierced us with her looks and plucked us with her words. She made us nervous, and she made us feel cheap. She tried so hard to close us out and to box him in. That boy of hers.

Now, I have this boy of mine. I've caught my breath this summer, looking at him, surprised that I have a son this old. Surprised that I have a son this handsome. Surprised that I have a hold so fleeting. It makes me sad to know I'll have to share him soon.

My watchful heart races as I sit in the lounge chair, hiding behind black Ray-Bans and pretending to read Oprah's latest pick. It's a romance, but it holds no interest. Instead, I am caught in the drama before me—the tiny bikinis, the flirtatious lilt, the warm sun in the days before junior high.

I know it's no accident that this parade of prepubescent girls marches past his towel or stands, just by chance, in the deep end where my son dives. I've heard their skittish breaths and stifled laughs on the other end of the phone. I've noticed their hands cover their mouths, hiding secrets their eyes can't help but reveal. They are, after all, in seventh grade. They are me.

Am I her?

Self-conscious that my hair is not in style or my suit not in fashion, I smile stiffly at one girl who passes my way. She hesitates, trying too hard to meet my glance. She's a cute little thing, a bit overweight and a bit under-height. But I like her, I think. Or at least I'll try.

My son shrugs when I ask him her name. Then slugs me—"Oh, Mom"—when I tell him to be careful.

He's growing up so fast. I sigh, going back to the book I can't seem to finish. "I'm sorry, Mrs. Sarti," I say to the words lined up on the page.

Judi Christy

The Sunny Side

At the back of my closet, on top of a box of homemade 78 rpm records, is a worn leather case containing a very old trumpet. The instrument once belonged to my mother. Opening the case, I touch the valves, stuck now after eighteen years of neglect, and the odor of brass and lubricating oil evokes a flood of memories.

The records, too, recorded long ago, recall precious days gone by. On some, my mother is singing to my piano accompaniment; on others, we're playing the numbers together, me on piano, she on trumpet. As I listen now to the two of us playing "Sunny Side of the Street," her favorite song and one that describes her outlook on life, I realize how much she meant to me.

"It's four o'clock, Gary. Time to practice!"

I dreaded hearing those words. I wanted to be outside playing baseball with my friends.

"You played a wrong chord, and you're not count-ing; your rhythm is way off, Son," she said from the kitchen, where she was preparing dinner. Mom came into the room holding a bowl of mashed potatoes and waving a wooden spoon like a conductor. "One, two, three. It's a waltz, Gary. It's three-quarter time."

Why couldn't I have a normal mother like other guys? A mother who let her boy play manly games after school rather than forcing him to sit behind this sissy instrument of torture for an hour?

Years later I regretted those thoughts and came to appreciate my mother more fully. But at age twelve, I felt encumbered by her prodding. Oh, I had heard my grandmother's stories about her remarkable daughter; I could recite them verbatim. But all that happened a long time ago. What did any of it have to do with now, with me?

Not that I didn't respect my mother's achieve-ments; I most certainly did. Had she been a stranger, I might even have been in awe of them. But to me, then, she was just my mother. I didn't see her as oth-ers saw her.

I didn't see her as the tiny three-year-old who had lost her left arm and left leg under the wheels of a trolley car. Or as the small child who tap-danced professionally with her sisters at the Curran Theatre in San Francisco. Or as the accomplished musician who, at the age of sixteen, became a member of the

San Francisco All Girl Symphony Orchestra. Or as the teenager who learned to drive a stick shift on the hilly streets of San Francisco. Or as the woman who inspired so many World War II amputees who watched her perform in hospitals and USOs.

Growing up, I didn't notice her struggle to perform simple daily tasks. I didn't even think back to the young mother who tied my shoes when I was a little kid. Have you ever tried to tie a pair of shoes with one hand? I saw only a mother who, for some reason, was possessed with the ridiculous notion that I learn to play the piano.

My mother became fascinated with the piano when she herself was twelve, after hearing Gershwin's "Rhapsody in Blue." Of course, playing the piano was out of the question for her. As a consolation, her father gave her a trumpet. It was to become her career. At first she struggled, but she soon became so gifted that she began to play professionally.

At nineteen, a follow-up story on her accident appeared in the *San Francisco Examiner*, where she was quoted as saying, "Nothing is impossible if you want it bad enough and go after it hard enough." Throughout a lifetime of adversity and struggle, my mother always managed to walk on that "sunny side."

My parents divorced after the war. Neither remarried. My dad visited on weekends, and I spent summer vacations with him, but it was my mom who shouldered the responsibility of raising me. She taught trumpet during the week and took to the stage on weekends. I vividly recall her coming home and limping into the bathroom to soak the open abrasions caused by standing and playing for hours. Yet, she never once complained.

Mom always wanted me to learn to play "Rhapsody in Blue." But shortly after she presented me with the student version, when I was fifteen and in my fifth year of practice, I quit playing piano. It came to a head one evening when she corrected a particularly bad chord. I got up, slammed the lid down over the keyboard, and turned to her, shouting, "I hate this piano, Mom! I've been practicing this thing for years, and I hate every minute of it. I'm sorry you have only one arm and can never play, but you're not *me*. I can't play *for* you!"

Her eyes grew suddenly misty, and then she nodded and quickly left the room. Within the week, the piano was gone. Kids can be cruel.

At seventeen, I joined the Navy, followed by my enlisting in the Army Special Forces. The training was rigorous, and many times I was tempted to quit. But then I would remember my mother's mantra: "Nothing is impossible if you want it bad enough and go after it hard enough."

Mom never asked whether I was playing piano. I did, of course, for I found that I could supplement my meager wages in those early years with tips from "sitting in" at nightclubs or piano bars. As time wore on, however, I quit playing altogether.

In time, I retired from the Army to our present home in Oregon, taking a job as an attendance officer at the local high school. Mom visited often, and much to her delight, I eventually bought a piano and started playing again.

The high school held an annual dinner-and-talent-show night. I was usually prevailed upon to play, and I did it solely for the kids. One year, though, I had an additional purpose in mind.

My wife, my mother, and I were sitting at a table when the curtain parted and the master of ceremonies announced, "We have a special treat for someone in the audience." At that, a soft light was focused on our table. "He has played piano in many places around the world, but he told me this will be his most memorable performance. He'd almost given up learning this very difficult piano solo until he remembered this motto: 'Nothing is impossible if you want it bad enough and go after it hard enough.'"

I laid my napkin down and gave Mom's hand a squeeze as I arose. Then I walked up the steps to the stage.

The lights dimmed and a blue spotlight shown on the piano as I began the first glissando of "Rhapsody in Blue." Tears of joy filled my mother's eyes and her fingers tapped the table to the rhythm of the music, reminding me not only of that wooden spoon so many years ago, but also of the tears I'd caused the day I quit. When I finished, I walked offstage and hugged her.

"Thank you, Mom. Thank you for being my mother."

Within a year, she was diagnosed with colon cancer. I held her as she sobbed. Ten months later and after a second operation, the doctors held little hope. Mom faced death with the same dignity with which she had faced life. She put her mortality behind her and never spoke of it again.

She was heavily sedated that last night in the hospital, but as I took her hand in mine, she still had the strength to grip it weakly. Then she looked at my wife and me and said simply, "Love each other." Those were her last words to us.

Through her living example, Mom gave me the tools to cope with life's difficulties. The obstacles that have crossed my path have been nothing compared with those she encountered each day of her life. Yet, through it all, she persevered and remained positive. That, then, is my mother's legacy: an indomitable spirit, reveling in song, striding purposely and graciously on the sunny side of the street. I'm doing my best to follow in her footsteps.

Gary B. Luerding

An Unexpected Truth

"You can use my big new glove, Mommy," the little boy said in short, excited breaths as he searched the room for his glove. He ran into the TV and apologized, "Oh, excuse me. Ha!" looking quickly to make sure his mother still stood in the door, waiting. He must not lose her. He found the glove under his bed and handed it to her, noting that she held it the way she always held his things, as if she expected to hand it back to him right away. But she wouldn't hand it back. Not today. Today, she was finally going to pitch to him.

As he ran to the closet to get his ball and bat, the bat fell to the floor with an oafish *thump, thump, thump,* and he grunted in agitation, bending to pick it up. He had so wanted everything to be quiet for his mother—no loud noises to cause her to flit away like a bird. He looked to her, and she smiled faintly, seeming somewhat amused by his excitement.

Danny Keith was his real name, but his mother had started calling him Keefer when he was just a baby, premature and brought home weighing four pounds. All his little friends had called him Keefer, too, until he started school and the teacher had called out his name off the roll like a trumpet blaring. By now, in second grade, about the only person to call him Keefer was his mother, and there was something warm about it that made him feel closer to her. He needed that desperately sometimes—the closeness—for his mother "wrote things" and always seemed just out of his reach. Even now as he held open the back door for her, she seemed not to notice, walking past him with a fixed gaze, holding the glove as though it were something that might spill.

Once outside, he took some practice swings with the bat, while his mother read the trees and the sky like a new book and breathed in the air deeply, closing her eyes. Sometimes he felt that she belonged more to the earth and sky than to him or to his father or to anything else—that if left to the elements long enough, she would dissolve into them without a trace. And she was always searching for what she called "Truths." She once said there were moments when she seemed about to know all Truths, only to have them slip away. He hadn't quite understood what she meant, but it had caused him to want to be truthful with her.

The late September sun was just warm enough

to make his scalp draw up and crawl like a caterpillar, and he leaned on the bat waiting for his mother, enjoying it. She had put him off all summer with vague promises, which he'd thought she'd never keep, but here they were together, about to play ball, and he cherished every moment, even the waiting.

"Ready, Keefer?"

His mother's voice startled him, a voice that sounded strange out there in the sun, like it belonged to someone besides his mother. No, he wasn't ready! Yes, he was! Oh, it didn't matter, for he would hit the ball hard and long for her, and then go bring it back so she wouldn't have to run after it. He didn't want her to tire of the game too quickly and go inside.

He ground himself into his stance, gripping the bat fiercely. She smiled at him and threw the ball like real pitchers she'd seen, bringing her right leg around and following through, only to have the ball go streaming over his head and to the right of him.

"That's okay, Mommy." He laughed and ran to get the errant ball. He would explain that throwing the ball wasn't easy when you hadn't practiced. He didn't want her to be discouraged. But when he came back with the ball, she was listening attentively to the dying leaves in the wind as they spoke of the fall or of the coming winter, or of some Truth that she strained to hear.

"You can pitch underhand if you want to, Mommy."

She brought herself back to him at the sound of his voice, and when he threw the ball to her, she forgot to close her glove on it, so that it dropped at her feet heavily. He ran to pick it up for her, but she bent to get it herself, and he hurried back to his batting spot, feeling somewhat confused. Then, before he had set himself to swing, she lobbed the ball past him, and he saw her turn away with searching eyes. He ran quickly on his short legs to pick up the ball before she could attach herself to something else.

"I'm sorry, Keefer. I'm just no good at this."

"No! It's okay, Mommy, really." He just had to hit the next one for her.

He threw the ball back to her, and she caught it with both hands, causing her to hurt one of the fingers on her ungloved hand. He ran to her. "You all right, Mommy? Let me see."

"I'm all right." She showed him the finger, and he bent to kiss it shyly before turning in a circle and dancing back to his spot with his mother's warm smile still on him.

This time he set himself to hit the ball out of sight, and he concentrated so hard on it that it blurred as it came toward him, and he cut the air with a mighty swing that took him off his feet. He sat on the ground in a pool of embarrassment, wondering if she were disgusted with him to the point of quitting.

"I'll get it this time, honey." She ran past him and

reached down to brush his head with her hand as she went. He reached up to touch that spot and thought how strange it was to see his mother run like that. She ran funny, and he loved her for it.

"I'll just bet you hit it this time," she encouraged, seeming to know how badly he needed to hit it for her.

He readied himself, and this time he could feel all the muscles in his body strain toward the ball as it cracked against his bat and sailed out of the yard and into the pine thicket across the road. He threw down the bat and caught his mother's proud smile as he called back to her, "I'll get it, Mommy. You wait there!" Knowing even as he said it, that he would lose her—knowing.

And when he returned with the ball, red-faced and heart racing, his mother stood twirling a leaf she had plucked from the box elder, and she seemed to be looking at something far away that only she could see.

"Mommy, could I hit just one more for you? Just one more?" He waited, looking up at her with his brown eyes. "Mommy?"

"Umm?" Her eyes sought his, but brushed past them without taking hold. "Another day, Keefer. Mommy will pitch to you another day, I promise. You're doing fine, just fine." And the leaf twirled in her hand, soaking up the energy, allowing her mind to go elsewhere.

He reached into his pocket and pulled out two sparkling rocks to give her. "Here, Mommy. These are for you for playing ball with me. You sure are a nice mother to do that. Do you think those're real diamonds in the rocks? They're for you, Mommy."

She let the twirling leaf slip through her fingers and bent to take the rocks from him. Then looking at him tenderly with shining eyes—brighter than diamonds—she dropped to her knees and pulled him to her, swaying back and forth like the trees in the September wind.

With his face held against his mother's soft hair, the little boy didn't understand. He had only wanted to make her happy—to thank her for playing ball with him. He hadn't meant to make her cry.

Betty Peterson

This story was first published as "An Unspoken Truth" in *Bluegrass Woman*, August–September 1980.

Crossing
the Boundary Waters

We searched the shoreline for the portage trail, paddling as close as we could to the bank. I picked up the map, already soggy on our first day out. I couldn't even figure out which lake we were on, let alone where the portage might be. This trip to the Boundary Waters, a region of lakes between the United States and Canada, was my high school graduation gift to my son, Blue. We liked outdoor adventures, but we were used to river canoeing, where you simply followed the current. I hadn't realized how difficult it could be to find your way in the Boundary Waters, where lakes and rivers threaded into one another.

After fifteen or twenty minutes of patrolling the lake's edge, Blue asked me to pass him the map.

"I think it's over there," he said, motioning toward a stand of trees.

"I don't see any trail there," I countered, "but let's give it a try."

We skimmed over the water. Under the trees, partly hidden by a huge rock, was the portage trail.

"You've found your calling," I shouted to Blue as we crunched into the graveled shore.

He grinned. "I made a good guess." He picked up the map and pointed to a thin black line. "Here's the next portage trail. If we cut across here at a diagonal, we'll hit it."

I stepped out of the boat. "The map is yours," I told him, hauling out my pack. "I'll head the canoe wherever you tell me to."

Blue folded the map, tucked it into his back pocket, and bent down to get his pack. Tall and gangly, he looked like he had grown another inch since yesterday. I couldn't quite believe that, in the fall, he would be heading off to college. Since my divorce four years earlier, he and I had been family for one another. Now, he was in the boundary waters, that space between adolescence and adulthood. I, too, was in the boundary waters, that space between parenting a teenager and parenting a young adult. And I was still learning how to stop looking over his shoulder, how to be in the boat with him and simply paddle.

As a team, Blue and I paddled easily, but portaging didn't go as smoothly. We tried various strategies: one person carrying the gear, the other shouldering the canoe; the two of us raising the canoe overhead, then returning for our gear. Twice I dropped my end of the canoe. Finally, we settled on each of us carrying a pack with the canoe at hip height between us. Before the trip, I had dreaded the portages, the awkwardness of stopping and starting, the sheer weight of the canoe. Maybe I was also afraid of seeming weak in the eyes of my son. What if I had to rest more often? Could I let him shoulder more of the weight?

Late in the afternoon of the second day, as Blue studied the map to choose a campsite, the sky clouded over and the wind picked up.

"Let's head for that island," Blue said, pointing far across the lake.

"Okay," I conceded reluctantly. The waves were rising, and the canoe rolled in the swells. "Let's get going."

We lifted our paddles and plunged them into the turbulent water. I could feel the power of our combined energy pushing against the wind. Paddling with all our might, we inched forward, battling waves taller than the canoe. I tried to keep us on course, but when the wind caught one side of the bow or the other, we veered sideways, water sloshing over the gunnels. Blue quickened the pace. I tried to match him, but I was wearing down. Terrified that we might capsize, I gripped my paddle harder and forced myself to keep going. When I heard thunder, I knew it was time to give up.

"Let's head back," I hollered.

I couldn't hear Blue's answer, but I dug my paddle in deep to turn us.

A wave hit us broadside and the canoe tipped crazily. "Stay with the boat if we go over," I shouted, not sure if Blue could hear me.

I saw Blue rising in front of me, the bow lifting out of the water. "Hold on!" I screamed.

Water poured over my feet. Blue dropped out of my sight as the wave hurled me upward. I lurched back, straining to keep my paddle twisted to turn us. Blue reappeared, hunched forward and paddling in quick gulps.

"Keep going," I yelled, the waves now pushing us from behind. "Try to ride the swell."

We stroked in a frenzy, trying to keep pace with the waves heaving us back to shore. My arms felt detached from my body. There was so much water in the boat I couldn't tell if we were still afloat. I closed my eyes, and then we grated against sand. Blue was already out, dragging the boat. Too tired to hop out and help, I let him pull me in. We were on land; nothing else mattered.

That was the high drama of the trip; the low drama centered on food. Years ago I'd led canoe trips, but I was out of practice at figuring out how much food we would need for a week's trip. As I packaged up crackers and peanut butter, I tried to imagine each meal, what we would need to fortify ourselves for the next leg of the journey. I also included snacks for each day: oranges, nuts, and fruit leather.

"How many packages of oatmeal do you want for breakfast?" I'd asked Blue.

"Two," he assured me.

"Let's see, five days, that would be ten packets," I muttered, thinking out loud. "One a day for me. Fifteen." It seemed like a lot of oatmeal.

As the days passed, the food supply dwindled rapidly. By midweek, we were out of snacks. On the final morning, we were down to two packets of oatmeal. I ate half of mine and gave the rest to Blue. For lunch he cleaned out the peanut butter jar with his fingers; all the crackers were gone. When we met a couple at the end of a portage munching on trail mix, Blue eyed them enviously. They offered to share with us, and he gulped down the nuts and fruit. I felt badly; I had underestimated how much energy we would need to paddle every day. The hunger pangs didn't bother me much; I drank a lot of water, and I'd learned over the years how to keep going on an empty tank, if necessary, but I was worried about Blue. He used energy at a faster rate than I did, and I wanted the trip to end on a positive note.

Blue didn't complain much. He just kept imagining what he would order for his first off-the-water meal. We had passed a restaurant on our way in that advertised thirty-some kinds of pie. As we paddled, he kept bringing up the pie.

"I think I'll order blueberry," he daydreamed as he pushed his paddle into the water, "or maybe peach." He was partial to fruit pies. "Continental cherry," he mused. "Wasn't that on the list? Apple-raspberry; maybe I'll have that, too."

"It sounds like you're already sitting down at the counter." I laughed. "Look at the map. We've got three lakes and two portages to go."

"I know exactly where we are," he reminded me. "I'm the navigator. Let's get going."

I resumed paddling, daydreaming about dry socks. I'd brought only three pairs, and they were soaked. I'd tried going without socks one day, but my heel had rubbed against my wet shoe on the portages, so I'd gone back to wearing them wet. One night I tried to dry a pair by the fire and succeeded in burning the toes off, so I was down to two pairs. The soles of my feet were permanently wrinkled. While Blue dreamed of pie, I dreamed of taking off my wet shoes and stretching out my toes to dry.

In spite of our hunger, or maybe because of it, our strokes were strong that final morning, our paddling rhythm falling into synch as soon as we hit the water. I loved the way our energies flowed together: the leaning forward, the long pull through the water, our paddles pushing up at the same time.

We fairly flew over the water; it felt like we could go on forever: dip, dip, and swing; dip, dip, and swing. Part of me wanted the trip to go on and on. In a few weeks, Blue would leave for college, his energy going one way, mine another. We wouldn't be paddling the same canoe anymore. He would be paddling his own boat, and I would be standing on the shore, waving and wishing him well.

We hit our pullout spot in midafternoon. As soon as we saw the beach, Blue poured on the power. While I would have preferred a slower leave-taking, I matched my stroke to his and soon we were hoisting the canoe onto the car. Blue asked if we could stop at the first store we found so he could get a snack; he still wanted to hold off a full meal until Betty's Pies.

"Sure," I said as I pulled out onto the road. It felt odd to be in a car again, moving without using our own muscles. I pulled into a tourist stand.

"I'll wait in the car," I said. "If I start eating now, I might not be able to stop."

"You sure you don't want anything?"

"I'm holding out for Betty's," I said, handing him a ten-dollar bill. "Get whatever you want."

As I watched him cross the parking lot, I realized that staying in the car wasn't really about food. I wasn't ready for our trip to end. I wanted to keep paddling as a mother-son team, and I wasn't sure when that might happen again. We had navigated our way through the boundary waters; now we would be separating. I was glad we had had this adventure together, and I was glad Blue would be going off to seek his own adventures, but I cried as I saw him disappear into the store. I would always be his mother, but what that meant was shifting.

I don't remember what he bought to eat. I remember thinking it wasn't much, maybe a granola bar or a pint of chocolate milk.

"Here," he said, handing me a small paper sack as he drew his long legs into the car.

"But I didn't want anything," I protested, unfolding the top of the bag.

As soon as I looked in, I laughed. It was a pair of socks, clean and dry—and bright pink. I peeled off my soggy, mud-streaked remnants, but even before I put on the new pair, I felt warm and dry. We had passed through the boundary waters. My son would be leaving soon, but he would return, and in that returning, we would find new ways of give-and-take, new ways of being connected as mother and son. And wherever I went, I could pull out the pink socks and warm my feet.

Carol Tyx

 Speaking Son-ese

I heard my eleven-year-old son before I actually saw him. The kitchen door banged against the wall. His backpack dropped to the floor with a heavy thud. His high-pitched, wait-till-you-hear-this voice called my name.

"Guess what I'm going to buy when I'm sixteen?" he half asked, half announced. Without waiting for a reply, he sped on. "An Eclipse. Then I'm gonna buy a body kit and tail, because they make it look better. Jesse's gonna get a Viper or maybe a Skyline. Have you seen the Enzo Ferrari? It's the fastest: zero to sixty in three-point-six seconds, six-hundred-sixty horsepower. But it's real expensive."

"Whoa, wait a minute," I threw in as he gulped a breath. "What are you talking about? Where did you see all these cars?"

"Jesse's house. We played 'Need for Speed'; that's a cool game. I had a Viper and got up to one-hundred-twenty miles per hour. Jesse beat me, though; he had the Ferrari. Where's Geoffrey?"

He bounded down the stairs, executed a jump over the bottom three steps, and asked his brother to guess which car he was going to buy. I sighed and reached for a cup of tea.

Nate has always shared his discoveries with me. As a preschooler, he cupped my face in his hands and eagerly recounted why the red car was his favorite. In those face-to-face moments, I could respond by simply nodding and saying, "Yes, that is a bright color." But this explosion of car talk is a foreign language. Though I had concentrated on his detailed explanation of "Need for Speed," I sensed I had just been left in the dust.

Where had he learned this new language?

I know that, in some homes, the car parked in the driveway is nearly always surrounded with spray bottles, rags, and containers of blue liquid; the hood propped open for inspection. In those families, "horsepower," "octane level," and "compression ratio" are spoken as casually as asking what's for dinner, and the children learn the lingo right along with their ABCs.

My husband and I are definitely not fluent in car talk. In our home, the owner's manual retains its glossy new-book glow because it is seldom opened. We're on a first-name basis with the service mechanics who patiently answer our frantic phone calls describing an engine that sometimes *kerplunk*s and sometimes *chink*s. We prefer singing "rain, rain go away, come again another day" while the car is propelled through the automated car wash to snapping a family photo of us washing the car together on some sunny afternoon.

On the other hand, when Nate was in preschool, our conversations consisted of "beep, beep," "honk, honk," and "vroom, vroom." I was much more articulate when Hot Wheels dominated our playtime. In fact, I think I was nearly as excited as he had been to build the loop-the-loop track and add soap and water to the mini car wash.

We spent hours on our knees, pushing the little ninety-nine-cent hot rods around the obstacle courses we had constructed of boxes and blocks. When we pulled up to the miniature McDonald's, we ordered our Chicken Nuggets Happy Meal and politely asked for extra ketchup. When we drove around town, we returned books to the library, turned on Fifth Street to go to church, and then headed south to school. When we raced around the track, our cars spun out of control and crashed into each other amid cries of "again, again!"

When he was in elementary school, the hours spent racing around the floor gradually gave way to hours spent building at the table with Legos. For a while, we raced with multicolored square block vehicles. Then his Lego creations turned intergalactic, and the Jedi Starfighter and Republic Gunship earned front-and-center positions on his dresser top. He parked the Hot Wheels on a shelf in the closet . . . and one day, put them in a box.

"I've grown out of them," he explained and, with no sign of regret, turned back toward his room.

"Wait. Let's not get rid of all of them," I called after him, picking up a bright red, silver-streaked racer. "This is one of your favorites, isn't it? Let's save it and pick out a few others. You might want them for a project some day."

He rolled his eyes and picked four cars from the box, and I added some of my favorites: the school bus, the hippie van, the purple pickup, the black Mercedes. After he returned to his room, I added a few more—the red convertible, the garbage truck, the No. 17 Firebird—and carefully placed each in individual car-sized compartments within an airtight plastic container. The rest I carried to the basement and tossed into a box marked "Garage Sale."

I boxed up more than some worn-out toys that day; I also boxed up a part of our relationship. I had sensed for some time that this change was coming. When he was in fourth grade, he'd bought his first poster: a yellow Porsche. A silver-blue Lotus Elise was soon hanging beside it on his bedroom wall. Then he began playing computer games that challenged his ability to maneuver a racecar through the twists and turns of the autobahn and through the streets of New York City. A year later, he was snapping together the plastic pieces of model cars, and the 1:43 scale replicas soon took over the center-front position of his desk, driving the Legos to a shelf in his closet.

Now, even the pictures he draws for Grandma's refrigerator are filled with roll bars and mag wheels. A racetrack is outlined with masking tape on his bedroom floor, simulating the hairpin turns of the video game speedways he has mastered. Tiny tires, hubcaps, and body tops—pieces to his 1:64 scale, radio-controlled Mazda RX-8—lie amid the papers on his desk, the owner's manual open to a description of how a power upgrade kit will improve its performance.

Frankly, I'm not the least bit interested in cars. I don't know the significance of rpms or the differences between methanol and nitromethane. I don't like to watch action movies that treat cars like Hot Wheels racers, and I think there are better things to do than sit in front of a television screen and push buttons on a four-inch video game controller.

But because Nate is interested in cars, I find myself sitting in the passenger's seat during our conversations.

"Did you see that Mustang? That's a cool car."

"You had a Mustang? Wow. What was it like?"

"Man, look at the muffler on that car!"

"Drive into that car lot, will ya, Mom? I think

that's a Civic Coupe."

All I have to do—all he really wants me to do—during these exclamations is to pay attention and listen. But sometimes it's hard to keep my eyes from glazing over, and I have to swallow a yawn or two while he goes on and on and on. Sometimes, I stare at his lips, thinking that if I can read as well as hear what he's trying to tell me, I'll understand it. At times, I even wish he was at his friend's house instead of in my car—but then I'm glad he's not.

That's when I know the checkered flag is in sight: He's still talking to me. Still including me in the winner's circle. Translating a bit of the young man he is becoming into words I can understand.

And believe me, he's got his work cut out for him.

Yesterday, when he ran into the house and dropped his backpack on the floor, his wait-till-you-hear-this voice was camouflaged with compound bows, quivers, twelve-gauge shotguns, and clay pigeons. I guess I should start looking for an orange vest.

Karna J. Converse

Can You Hear Me Now?

I am the mother of a son who marches to the beat of his own drummer. Undaunted by convention and oblivious to the edicts of others, he goes along his merry way, leaving behind a trail of frustration for those less maverick in their approach to life. I love this unregimented kid; I know he loves me. We usually understand each other. Being somewhat irreverent myself, I have tried to nurture and encourage his independent spirit during our twenty-three years together. At the same time, I must admit to sometimes trying to program him to think the way I do. I haven't always been successful—much to his credit.

This somewhat contradictory dynamic of our relationship clearly presented itself during his sophomore year in college. Mother's Day was approaching, and I had my heart set on spending some of the day with him. Since Jordan's school was only two hours away, my husband and I hoped to drive up on Sunday morning to spend a day laughing, sharing stories, and bonding with our son, and then head back in the early evening. Like the mother-of-an-adult-son I was trying to be, I left it up to Jordan to call to arrange our Mother's Day visit. When I hadn't heard from Jordan by the middle of the week, I called him.

"Hi, honey. Dad and I were thinking of coming up for Mother's Day and spending some time with you. How does that sound?" Hearing only breathing, I continued. "How does ten or eleven o'clock sound?"

Silence. *Was the phone dead?* I clicked it once or twice.

"Well, I don't know, Ma," he said hesitantly. "My roommate is having some friends from Maine sleep over this weekend, so could you come later in the day, like at four or five, or better yet, how about six or seven?"

Trying not to sound disappointed, I stooped to the old "blame Daddy" trick while levering with the old "Mommy manipulation" device.

"You know, honey, Dad likes to be home before midnight on Sundays so he can organize himself for work on Monday."

No counteroffer. *What, was he brain dead?* Clearly I was being blown off, which didn't please me, but I also realized his dilemma. So, I revised the offer and tried to act like the adult.

"You know what, Jords, since you'll be busy Sunday, why don't I come up next week, on a weekday, and spend some time with you then?"

God would surely reward me for my sacrificing countenance.

"That sounds great. Thanks, Mom."

Satisfied, he hung up. Less than satisfied, I waited for him to call back and apologize for his priorities faux pas. The call never came. And I was more than a little put out with my "baby boy." *Had he learned nothing from me?*

Five o'clock Sunday morning, Mother's Day, found me in bed, eyes open, staring at the ceiling, pondering the unhappy turn of events, weighing my needs against my son's needs. I kept hearing my own mother's voice echoing in my head. Her child-rearing theory was, "If you don't teach them, nobody will." Decision made, I dressed and headed downstairs to confront my husband.

"Honey, would you like to go up with me to Jordan's school this morning?"

"No, thanks," he quietly replied. But he clearly meant, *What, are you out of your mind?* He has excellent survival instincts.

"Well, I'm going," I announced.

Meekly, he asked, "Isn't it a little early?"

Blinded by my mission, I said, "No, I don't want to hit traffic."

"What traffic? It's six o'clock Sunday morning. . . ."

I heard his voice trailing off as I headed out the door.

I parked in front of Jordan's dorm at eight o'clock on the dot. *Okey-dokey; now what?* This was as far as I'd gotten with my plan. I sat outside in the car for about twenty minutes, waiting anxiously for someone, anyone, to come out of the house so that I could send him back in to wake Jordan. Realizing I could be waiting out there as long as I had waited for Jordan's come-to-his-senses phone call, I headed up the stairs.

The door was open. In the room were about seven people, sleeping all over the place. Crawling over a lovely blond girl, I struggled for my balance as I murmured, "Excuse me. Pardon me." Faced with her curious gaze, I whispered, "It's okay, go back to sleep. I'm Jordan's mother."

"Cool," she yawned and turned over.

"Excuse me, pardon me," I whispered again, stepping over a tall boy sprawled out in the center of the room.

"Sure," he smiled, snuggling up to his pillow.

Nice kids; I could tell they were brought up well. So, why weren't they with their mothers today? But not my problem. I had other issues to address.

I finally got to Jordan and nudged him lightly on the shoulder. "Jordan, Jordan."

He rolled over, opened his eyes, and not the least

bit surprised, he smiled and said, "Oh, hi, Ma."

"Jordan, please come out with me," I motioned to the door.

After we crawled across the people, the clothing, the guitars, the food containers, and the bottles, we sat on the couch out on the porch.

"So, honey, how are you?" A ridiculous question, when it was rather clear how he was—hung over and exhausted. "I suppose you're wondering what I'm doing here?"

Pause. "Yeah, Ma, what are you doing here?"

"Well, I felt that it was important for me to make a point today."

"At eight o'clock in the morning?" he slurred. "We got to sleep at five."

"Time is not the issue here," I continued, unfazed. "What matters is that you learn something today about priorities."

"Uh-huh."

I was definitely losing him. "If I don't teach you, no one will, Jordan. . . . Jordan?"

"Not that again, Ma. Teach me what?" His eyes closed, his body molded into the couch.

"Today is Mother's Day, and I wanted to spend some time with you."

His eyes opened slowly. "Ma, I don't believe in all these hyped-up holidays. I don't believe in Mother's Day."

"You know, it's a funny thing," I said, my voice rising for effect, "They don't call it 'Jordan's Day.' They call it 'Mother's Day.' And I do believe in it!"

I was going for the homerun now. "So, I made this four-hour round-trip so that you would understand just how important it is to me."

"Uh-huh." He was disappearing into the couch again.

I was not making the impact I had counted on.

"Okay, Jordan, I'm going to leave now, but I want you to remember this for the future. There are people in this world other than just you."

I made a gesture to leave and realized there was no groundswell for me to stay. "Bye, honey."

"Bye, Ma. I love you." I heard his body collapse into the cushions.

I walked out, went to my car, started the engine, and drove away. Five minutes down the road, reassessing the situation, I realized I had accomplished nothing. Worse, he probably would think he dreamt the whole thing. Back I went. I had not gotten what I had come for: special time spent with my son.

This time I was more familiar with the terrain. I went back into the room, stepped over the same kids—"Excuse me, pardon me"—tapped Jordan on the shoulder and woke him again. He was no more surprised this time than the time before. When I asked him about it later, he calmly said that he knew

I'd come back and was just trying to catch some more sleep before I did.

We had a wonderful couple of hours. We went to breakfast and ordered exactly the same thing, as we often did: scrambled eggs, loose, with a well-done English muffin, dry. We spoke about the family, his feelings about school, what he was doing, and who he was meeting. After a while, I brought him back to get some more sleep, so he could carouse with his friends later that day.

I came to teach him lessons, and hoped that I had. I'd learned some too—one of them being to ask for what you need. Not a bad life lesson to pass along to an up-and-coming adult.

By the way, the following year on Mother's Day, Jordan was in Prague as an exchange student. At eight o'clock that morning, on the dot, New York time, the phone rang.

"Hi, Ma. Happy Mother's Day."

He had heard me, after all.

Linda Holland Rathkopf

The Anole Story

I am an unusual female. I hate to shop. I make my way through a department store or, heaven help me, a mall only when I am in serious need of clothes for an upcoming event or vacation. Even then, it is a solo pursuit. Unlike my mother, I never call a friend to go shopping for the sheer pleasure of it. Browsing is not a part of my repertoire.

As if the normal contrariness of teenagers wasn't enough, to torture me even further, my two daughters had to pick shopping as the mother-daughter bonding activity of their choice. Now that they're grown and gone, our bonds secure from all that shopping, I relish the prospect of never having to accompany another loving soul into a building that houses a cash register. The two males in my household, my husband and sixteen-year-old son, despise shopping. My son is on the forefront of a new generation that buys everything online.

But recently, new driver's license in pocket, he is on the lookout for errands to run. Today, this brings him out of his room, where he has been holed up for the past two years with the door closed, and into my kitchen, a bit more conversational than the monosyllabic replies I generally receive when I ask about his day. He wants to go for new sneakers, which he desperately needs, and then he wants to buy an anole.

An anole, he explains, is an awesome reptile that eats live crickets, and you can watch its throat swell as it swallows them whole.

This is not on my list of interesting attractions, although from the animated tone of my son's voice, it is clearly on his. The bonding opportunities looming on the horizon appear so limited. Perhaps this is why I, who have been known to fake a coma to avoid accompanying one of my girls on a shopping trip (unsuccessfully, I might add), find myself asking, "Do you want company?" After a moment of respectful hesitation (or is it shocked silence?), he says, "Sure."

My son shops with a mission, like I do. He tackles the shoe store, a discount outlet with rows of stacked boxes where you figure out your own size, tie your own laces, and don't have to deal with a salesperson. Within twenty minutes, we are back on the sidewalk, new sneakers on his feet. Together, we try to remember how long it's been since he's bought a new pair. I feel our bonds tightening.

Before we get to the pet store, I must interject that I've never liked reptiles. In this I think I'm a typical female. Through the years there have been the requisite goldfish and hermit crabs, the captured box turtles and caterpillars (all spun cocoons, and one actually emerged as a monarch butterfly)—creatures the children could confine to their rooms and thereby call their own. I drew the line at birds and small, furry, caged animals, which would have provided little more than a feeding trough for the two family cats, and anything without legs that was cold-blooded (think slither).

It only goes to reason, then, that here in the super-store of all pet stores, past the rows of confined cats, the gallons of fish tanks, and the miles of bird cages, inside a gigantic terrarium chock full of rocks and twigs and leaves, awaits the critter my son now wished to call his own.

Peering through one of the glass enclosures, he pronounces, "This is them."

Them? A minute or two of steady gazing reveals the well-camouflaged anoles. They are appealing enough creatures, even for reptiles, about the size of my pinkie, not counting their tails, which are skinny and tapered and longer than their bodies. While I continue to gaze, my son wanders off and returns with another creature, a puffy, pale-faced individual

I hesitate to call our salesman. Despite the button on his shirt declaring him a "pet expert," he knows less about anoles than my son and he hasn't a clue how to catch one. He thrusts his pale hand in and around the terrarium in pursuit of the anole my son had selected, repeatedly grabbing at air.

My son, restraining a belly laugh, says, "It doesn't matter. Any two anoles are fine."

Two anoles? While I let this sudden population explosion sink in, the anoles still gleefully jump about, evading capture. The pet guy finally concedes he has been outsmarted by creatures with an IQ of maybe ten and goes for help. Another "pet expert" captures two anoles and puts them in a box.

"I don't have an environment," my son says.

For the record, an "environment" consists of equipment that is six times more expensive and occupies at least a thousand times more room than two anoles. We load up with one terrarium, which is far larger than two tiny anoles could possibly need for life support, some brown shredded stuff to line the bottom, a heat lamp and misting bottle to create tropical temperature and humidity conditions, a thermometer for obvious reasons, fake leaves for the anoles to seek shelter beneath when it gets too hot, and thirteen live crickets for their first meal.

"Make sure you feed them twice a week," the pet guy says.

I stare at the clear plastic bag, blown up like a balloon, thirteen crickets bouncing around inside, and cringe.

"Do you have to keep making faces?" my son says.

Later, after he has set up the whole thing in his bedroom, he mentions something I should have thought about earlier.

"I know this one's a male," he says, pointing to the vivid green one.

"How do you know?"

"See how he puffs his throat out and makes it turn red?" Gesturing toward the other, a duller gray creature, he adds, "But I'm not sure about that one."

I watch the green one, its throat puffing madly, make its way toward the gray one.

"I will never forgive you if they begin to mate."

"I think the males fight," he says.

The two of us draw our faces to the glass to better see which activity these two are about to engage in. Let's hope anoles eat their young.

Peggy Duffy

Roller Coaster Ride of Love

Nothing makes my mother's heart flip-flop like a ride on a roller coaster than the love I feel for my boys. When a chubby hand with dirt ground under the fingernails and Scooby Doo Band-Aids wound around the knuckles reaches up to seek mine as we walk down the sidewalk, there goes my heart, crazily looping around a curve. And when my boys stop crashing their dinosaurs into each other long enough to crawl over and give me an unexpected, sloppy kiss, there it goes again, full throttle down the track.

This roller coaster ride of mine starts off each morning sometime around dawn. I roll over with the eerie feeling that I am being watched. Sure enough, there they stand, with somber eyes still crusty from sleep, imploring me to scoot over so they can plunge under the covers. As they lay on either side of me, legs entwined in mine, I breathe in their sleepy boy smell, reminiscent of sweet rolls fresh out of the oven. Instead of sleeping, I remain in that delicious half-sleep state, relishing their apricot skin nuzzled against mine. With a thrill, I feel myself pitching down the first stomach-tingling fall of the ride.

Then they launch out of the covers like torpedoes, refreshed for another day of bouncing, kicking, punching, running, and fighting. After a morning of homemade pancakes that two boys insist must be shaped into stars, the aroma of maple syrup mixes into their boy smell, and it is just about good enough to eat. The mad chase ensues to scrub their pink faces and to lasso those stubborn cowlicks into cooperation before wrestling their wiry bodies into their clean jeans and striped shirts. I stand back to admire them—they look like two fresh-faced kids from a fifties television show. My heart is lurching up the incline, thumping with anticipation of round two on this amusement park ride.

The day is a whirl of romps at the park, bike rides, scuffed knees, playing catch, and building Lego towers. I spend hours just watching them play and jabber.

"Let's pretend we're building a cave," my older son calls out as he raids the linen closet for blankets to stretch out over their twin beds.

"Yeah, less pwetend we're monstuhs in a cave," replies my younger son in his wet, baby voice.

I am mesmerized by their movements as they pull their toys under their makeshift cave top. They busily bend and reach for things, and I watch their thin muscles move under their skin, their concentration punctuated by widened eyes and the licking of lips. I reach over and touch their silky cheeks and tousled hair, and they don't even notice.

Then, with a wicked smile, I bend over on all fours and growl my way into the fabric cave, where peals of boys' squeals erupt like a volcano, laughter that bubbles up heartily from the depths of their spirit. As I lash out with my monster claws and teeth, they continue to squirm and cackle, and the cave is a froth of skinny elbows and knees as I tickle them mercilessly until we lay in a worn-out heap, both of the boys sprawled on my torso, fighting over who has the softest spot. My heart prepares itself for another soar down the rickety track.

We gather in the kitchen for a refreshment break, and we impulsively decide to make Grandma's recipe for sugar cookies. They take turns licking the spoon and rolling out the sweet dough, their clownish lips lined in cookie batter, cheeks powdered with flour. They make massive decorations over the white icing of their cookies, emptying my small bottles of sprinkles. After long draughts of cold milk, I smile to see the peach fuzz over their lips outlined with a fresh white moustache. Then, they jet outside with renewed energy, me breathing hard to keep up with them. I brace myself for the wildest ride yet.

We clamber along boulders, prying them up to peek for bugs, worms, and slugs. We are lucky today; we have spied a large black beetle. My sons prod it along with a stick, like a circus lion. Sitting on a large rock, I watch them, and time seems to float away on the wings of the lazy butterfly that passes my shoulder. The fluttery leaves of spring frame the background. The smell of earth and fresh green things blends in with their sun-warmed skin.

"Look how pretty my new flowers look," I point out.

My older son looks up in his matter-of-fact way and says, "They don't look as pretty as you do."

I swoon and catch him up in my arms for a big kiss. He glows proudly as if he knows he did something right. I barrel up the loop with that delirious feeling that I'm almost going to fall out.

I check on the boys as they bathe after dinner. They spend an entire hour in the bathtub pretending they are scuba divers, pirates, and fishermen. I am thankful they are not surfers tonight, as this requires the creation of massive waves that spill over the sides of the tub, flooding the bathroom. Their wet, glistening skin reminds me of slippery seals. They laugh, gargle water, and spit out streams, then stretch out full-length on their stomachs, chattering constantly.

I approach them with the shampoo bottle, and they scream like girls caught in a thunderstorm.

"My eyes sting!" the youngest cries out, as he does every night.

I towel off their bodies, which now smell of water-melon soap, and wrap them up in fluffy towels. They fly off with a last burst of energy, and my heart takes another clankety roll down the track.

They are bundled up in clean, warm pajamas, a stripe of clean skin edged with a red band of Spider-man underwear peeking through. I stretch out in the middle of one twin bed, the boys balanced on either side of me. I read *The Cat in the Hat* while they hang on each word, reminding me when I misread a sentence.

"Is the Cat in the Hat in weal life?" my younger son asks.

"No, he's not. Cats don't talk," says my older son very seriously.

As I put down the book and turn off the light, I hum a song.

"Not that one, the horsey one," dictates my sleepy son.

I am familiar with his favorite lullaby, the one I've been singing for a thousand nights. I start humming it, "When you wake, you will find/all the pretty little horses."

My older son wedges his back against me, making

sure not to leave an inch of space between us. My younger son wraps his chubby arms around my neck. Before long, I hear the deep, long breaths of sleep take them over.

The day has ended pretty much like all the others that have come before it for the past five years. Just like the days that will follow. But I know these days are limited, as precious as those locks of fine blond hair pressed in their baby scrapbooks. Soon, those hands won't reach up to seek mine. There will be no more early-morning visits to my bedside and wet, honest kisses. But I also know this long roller coaster ride will continue, even if it slows down a bit. Every time my eyes rest on them, I know that the same little boy spirit will love their mother, and I will feel my heart slip and slide as I fall down the track.

Sharon Palmer

A Gracious Thing

Y ou pointed to a sign: "3/4 Violin for Sale—$75."
I added ten bucks to your lawn-mowing money,
and we drove south of town to where, it turned out, a
red-haired girl from your class lived. Going home, you
balanced the black case on your knees like a trophy.

Wednesdays, we'd hop into the red Datsun and
zigzag over to a gray-shingled house off Seventeenth
Street. Kids with fiddles and banjos gathered in a
kitchen that was pure Norman Rockwell. African
violets on the windowsill. Rooster salt and pepper
shakers on a fifties Formica table, an oversized American Legion calendar flowered with U.S. flags. In the
middle of the room sat white-haired Bill Butler, keeping time with his cane, while kids tapped out beats
on the marbled blue linoleum. No sheet music, just
squawking and plinking bluegrass tunes by ear.

That fiddle eventually got sold to little Eric next

door so that you could get a banjo. It felt so heavy. Throughout autumn and winter evenings, I cooked to the rhythm of *plinkety-plinks*. Suppers got on the table in record time.

Your first public performance. I sat with other parents on hard bleachers, inhaling a mixture of sweat and rubber. Below me in ceaseless motion were blurs of white shirts and swirls of black skirts, setting up and tuning instruments.

When you first told me you were picked to play a solo, I teased you.

"Remember near the end of *The Music Man*, when Robert Preston conducts the kids? And a mother stands up and yells, 'Play to me, Son!' That's what I'm gonna do."

"Mom!"

You warmed up the crowd with "Cripple Creek," and then you had them stompin' and clappin' to "Foggy Mountain Breakdown." We played in duet that night, Son, you on banjo and me on a harp of swelling heart strings.

Then one night while grading papers, my ears picked out muted, mellow sounds:

"Go tell Aunt Rhody . . . Go tell Aunt Rho-o-dy . . ."

Suspicious, I called out, "Ben, is your homework done?"

"I'm doin' it, Mom," you said as I zipped into your

bedroom in time to catch you snatching up a text-book—upside down.

Hammering beats soon exorcized Aunt Rhody's ghost. Raw, jarring notes that fit the abrupt shift in our lives. You played on borrowed guitars at school assemblies. I snatched minutes to stand behind the last row, at sea in the pounding bass and the chorus of swaying, shrieking bodies. When you'd bused enough tables at the Stardust, you bought your own guitar. Still no money for lessons.

Change quickened our beat. I counted time spent with you and your brothers in minutes instead of hours. After school, you headed to work to pay off your guitar. I added night school classes so I could pay bills. Even the red Datsun kept quitting on us.

Senior year, the Eagles moved in with us. Embedded in embers of my memory are songs that you played night after night: "Most of us are sad. . . . No one lets it show. . . ." Even now, I remember the lyrics, but still don't know the titles. Sometimes, late at night, I'd catch the drift of my old *Take Five* Brubeck LP.

At some point, I noticed that the guitar stayed, didn't lead to something else. Later, it hit me that somehow you'd reached out beyond me, that your instrument eased the ache of your inward void. And that when guitar had become Father to the son, I'd missed the beat.

After high school, you entered a trial by fire in smoke-shrouded, beer-drenched bars, like Nadine's and Rusty's and others. I lost count. There, the music was pitted against pinball machines, pool tables, blaring television sets. Playing to men in baseball caps with "Shit Happens" logos and to women poured into 501s and "What You See Is What You Get" T-shirts stretched over busty chests.

A middle-aged groupie, I followed one band after another. "Rock 'n' Roll" drifted into "Misled," then "South Pass," then "Junxion." "Off and Running" took you on the road to towns I had to look up on a map. Months later, you came home talking about good ol' boys suspiciously eyeing your long hair and earring. About sleeping in drafty basements under the bar and eating frozen pizzas straight from the carton. "Money in yer pockets, boys, and room 'n' board fer a week. We'll feed ya good." Sure.

One Saturday over coffee . . .

"Where is this leading? You're just spinning your wheels."

You struggled for words. "The day Ken showed me his guitar, showed me the chords, I could see it all; it all came home to me."

"Okay, then. I have my share of the money from the house. I want you to use it for that music school you told me about."

"Are you sure? I know you want me to go to college."

I shrugged. "This way, later on, you won't always wonder. Anyway, either it will take or you'll get it out of your system."

It took. In your distracted small talk. In absent-minded fingering of the strings. In notes dancing in your brain. In hastily scrawled letters arrived from California.

"Music theory gives shape to all those tinkering notes I've got in my head. I'm writing a piece that sounds so Italian, it reminds me of Grandma. I'm calling it 'Song for Rose.'"

I mailed you back a passage from *The Grapes of Wrath*:

*And perhaps a man brought out his guitar. . . .
And he sat on a box to play, and everyone in the
camp moved slowly in toward him, drawn in toward
him . . . and their minds played in other times, and
their sadness was like rest, like sleep . . . And each wished
he could pick a guitar because it is a gracious thing.*

After music school, you moved uptown. Trendy bars like Sandpiper and Jake's. Raw wood sun decks, hanging plants. Waitresses in Birkenstocks, their trays slung casually against Patagonia shorts. Yuppies eye-stalking through thin, filmy smoke, huddled around pitchers of margaritas. Watching Monday Night Football, bantering about powder snow. Blatantly oblivious, politely irksome.

I wanted to shout, "This is not Musak!" So it goes.

I'm sitting in a school again. In the recital hall of the performing arts center of a large university. Smoke-free, no drunks bleating out trite requests. Around me, people chat quietly, patiently waiting to hear good jazz. As the lights dim, a hushed expectancy ripples like a soothing balm. In the darkened quiet, my eyes pick you out as the musicians enter from stage right.

Play to me, Son.

Rosalie DiMichele Ferguson

Chaos Theory of Teenage Boys

I should have been suspicious when my thirteen-year-old son asked me—his mother, the writer—to be the advisor for his robotics team. Instead, I was so flattered I said yes. At an age when most boys would rather don a tutu than spend time with Mom, I felt truly blessed that my son wanted me. An intelligent woman would have remembered what happened the previous two times her son asked her to do something with him.

First, it was an invitation to go on a Boy Scout camping trip. William had been in Scouts for a year and allowed his dad to go on many of the trips. I waited somewhat patiently to be wanted, too. When my turn came, I jumped at it without question. Big mistake.

"So, where are we going?" I asked in all innocence.

"Donner Pass."

"In January? Won't there be snow?"

"That's the point."

"There's room in the cabin for parents?"

"We're snow camping, Mom."

"So, there's another mom I can bunk with?"

"I don't think any other mothers are going. You'll need your own tent."

"Tent?"

"We're *snow* camping, Mom."

I finally got the point. Hike into the snow, pitch tents in the snow, cook in the snow, do everything in the snow. For three days. At Donner Pass.

Now, I'm the kind of gal who is quite comfortable in the great outdoors—in spring, summer, and fall. I'm also the kind of gal who puts on her down parka when the mercury drops to 65 degrees. "Isn't Donner Pass the place where that wagon train got stuck and all those people froze to death?" I asked.

"Yeah. Cool, huh!" said my son.

It took me two weeks to build up the courage to wimp out on my first Boy Scout camping invitation, but I finally did. My son took it in stride, parlaying my guilt into a promise to go river rafting instead. The most memorable part of that adventure was not bobbing down the American River and getting soaked with water cannons aimed at my face for the better part of four hours, nor was it being steered under the thorny blackberry bushes that crept along the bank and snagged my new bathing suit. It was supervising dinner production.

In Boy Scouts, I discovered, the boys are supposed to do everything. The adults' job is to make sure they don't permanently maim themselves while doing everything. Supervising dinner is no different: The boys do the cooking; the adults do the observing and eating. I never knew observing anything could be so difficult or unappetizing. Let's just say that finding a blue streak of Gatorade in your reconstituted mashed potatoes is not as disconcerting as the odd crunchiness of the same.

So, when William decided to head a team participating in a robotics competition hosted by The Tech Museum of Innovation in San Jose, California, and asked me to be the team's adult advisor, I hesitated briefly.

"But I don't know anything about robotics," I protested.

"That's why you'll be good. You won't take over the project."

I chose to accept his reasons for wanting me as a compliment. And he was correct; I didn't take over the project. I soon realized that my role was not so much to advise as it was to perform crowd control. Taking five seventh-grade boys out of the school setting and presenting them with a project is like . . . well, like nothing I'd ever experienced, although I am reminded of the pack of velociraptors in *Jurassic Park*. They communicate through a series of grunts, and their number-one objective is food. More meeting time was devoted to the procurement and consumption of snacks than to any other item.

"How are you going to attach the wheels to the chassis?" I'd ask.

"You gonna eat that cupcake?"

"Hey, you already had two cupcakes."

Being a good advisor, I'd bring them back on track. "Gentlemen," I'd say in a very authoritative tone, "how are you going to attach the wheels to the chassis?"

"I want sprinkles. Andy brought sprinkles."

Besides food, I found my team was obsessed with things that stick or flame. It seems you can't have too much duct tape. It sticks to fingers, mouths, and clothing, and if you ball it up and launch it at someone, it will stick to hair, too. Oh, and sometimes it even sticks to something mechanical.

Another favorite was Super Glue. The answer to the question, "How are you going to attach . . . ?" was always Super Glue. That was until the grandfather of one of the boys loaned him a propane torch and taught him to solder—something that both involves flames and makes things stick. Talk about a miracle device! How do you attach the peg to the frame? Solder it. How do you attach the nut to the bolt? Solder it.

Oops, did I say nut? Try saying "nut" and "screw" in the same sentence amid a pack of thirteen-year-old boys. Their intellectual powers shut down as they snort and guffaw and poke each other in the ribs. I tried saying, "Who has that threaded octagonal thing that screws onto the end of the bolt?" but darn, I used the "s" word, and all coherent thought was lost for another ten minutes.

My experience as a robotics team advisor taught me a few valuable lessons about working with teens, including the universal importance of snacks, the drawing power of fire, and that "twist" is an adequate synonym for "screw." I also learned that when you torch a Tootsie Roll, it melts and hardens into a miniature puck. How did I discover this phenomenon? By learning that if you leave boys alone for even one minute with a propane torch and a Tootsie Roll, they will experiment. I still haven't figured out what this has to do with robotics.

What was the outcome of this grand experiment? I got to witness Andy discover that he might one day want to lead his own team, Matt channel his Lego abilities into a real design achievement, Bradley infuse every meeting with his exuberant spirit, Terry calm arguments with his positive attitude, and William solve complex engineering problems in his head. I got to witness the boys, *my* boys, operate their robot successfully in front of a panel of judges. And I got to witness them win the award for the Most Courageous Team—an award they earned partly because they took on me, a nonengineer, as their technical advisor and managed to succeed anyway.

There is talk of building hovercrafts in my backyard next. I'm bringing the snacks.

Susan Sleman Hare

This story was first published in the *Christian Science Monitor*, April 24, 2003.

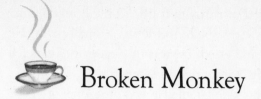 Broken Monkey

In this moment, I find peace from this trying day. My little monkey tried to climb and fell from the sky. He broke his arm. He sleeps now. This day was hard, but now I have my little boy back for a time. I have missed him. He's become so independent, always wanting to do things all on his own. Look Ma, no net. He is already going into his kindergarten classroom by himself. Just walks up those steps with his little backpack. Says hello to the teacher. I have to wait at the sidewalk. He wants to be big and strong.

I didn't see the fall. Only heard the scream. Blood really does run cold. His arm looked so strange. It had two wrists. There he was on the rubber ground under the jungle gym, screaming in pain. He weighs 50 pounds, but I didn't even notice. I scooped him up and ran with him, calling to my other children to keep up. For once, they were chasing after me.

As I sailed us through traffic to the hospital emergency room, I thanked God it was a small town. He whimpered and cried. He was in such pain. Tears fell from me. My oldest cried in sympathy.

It was no one's fault. It was just one of those things. There was no stopping it. I was half a play yard away. Who would think he would crash to the ground? How many other times has he fallen to earth? I could never count all those other times he fell without a scratch. Then, today, he has two broken bones. What's a mom to do?

It was just a little busy in the ER. We didn't have to wait long. The room was small for all of us: me, my broken one, and my two other sons. I focused on Brandon, looking him in the eye. The noises from the other boys just washed around me. They vied for attention, both trying to move the focus from Brandon, not understanding Brandon's need. Brandon looked to me to fix it. Looked to me to take away the pain. To whisk it away with a swish of my hands. Magic mom, make it all a dream.

He even spoke his wish. "I wish this was a dream, so I could wake up," he said. To wake up and have it not be true. To have the pain, the fall, be nothing more than a passing bad dream. I wished I could make it so.

The nurse came into our room. It felt better to have help. The doctor would arrive soon to set the bone, but the nurses were already there. I relinquished the pressure of having to know what to do. They gave him a liquid pain medication. It was an immense relief to see the pain ebb away from my little guy, to see him relax and rest. We had to wait for the swelling to go down a bit before the doctor could set the bones.

First, they took him to X-ray. And the worst began. He had to hold his arm in the right position for the picture. It hurt to hold it that way. He wanted to cradle it. He screamed and moved when the technician let go. Another try. He held still until the technician was behind the shield—then, another move. Again reposition. Finally, a good one, and off we rolled to our room and the brothers.

More liquid dreams were given. My boy faded to sleep. The other two got cabin fever and tried to take off on the spinning doctor's stool. The nurses found a children's video, and the boys watched TV in the nurses' office while I watched Brandon sleep.

The doctor appeared. Said it was a simple break involving two bones in Brandon's arm. He could set it, as soon as the anesthesiologist got there. Brandon needed to be under full anesthesia, but, hopefully, would need no surgery. It all depended on whether the doctor was able to pop the bones back into place.

I stood in the hall outside the treatment room. I moved to my boy's side, touched his hair and face.

I answered questions about weight, allergies, and health conditions. Finally, the sweet dreams doctor told my boy he will go to sleep and when he wakes up his arm will feel much better. The IV started, I kissed his forehead, and he did sleep. The two doctors waited, sitting on stools and watching vital signs. I returned to my post in the hall. I watched them watch my boy's heartbeat and breathing on the monitors.

Then, the orthopedic surgeon looked at me and asked if I was sure I wanted to watch him set the bone. It won't be pretty.

"I'm fine," I said. "Do it."

My heart stopped. *He's trying to pull my son's arm off!* I kept telling myself that Brandon would never know. He didn't feel the pain. The doctor stood and kicked his stool. He muttered to himself. I heard him say: "Come on, kid. Move. No surgery today."

The doctor tried to leverage the bone. A grown man using all his strength to move two little bones. Finally, the bones moved. One instant, the arm's broken. The next, it looks like nothing bad happened today.

The doctor's shoulders dropped and relaxed. He looked up, closed his eyes, took a deep breath, and looked at me. He said, "I think I got it. One more X-ray to make sure, but I don't think I'll have to pin it."

Now, I could breathe again. I got to take my baby home. Four hours after we arrived, we all left the ER.

My boy is now asleep on our comfy, old over-stuffed chair. It's the story chair; Mom's comfort chair. There he sleeps. Time will heal him. Dried tears shine on his round checks.

For now, he's my little boy once again. A little boy dreaming in natural sleep, with no drugs to keep him there. I'll move him to my bed soon. I'll watch over him tonight like he was a baby, fresh and new.

Tomorrow, I'll have to keep him from climbing and running. Once the arm heals, I'll be the one afraid as he climbs. I'll have to practice the frozen smile. I'll use it when he shouts, "Look, Mom! I'm at the top of the monkey bars." I'll smile around my heart and say, "I see you. You are a great little monkey."

Mary Paliescheskey

Some Distance
Now Required

Somewhere between finishing sixth grade and starting seventh, my only son transformed from a sweet little boy into a standoffish young man. Okay, maybe "standoffish" is a little harsh, and in truth, he was merely a teenage boy coming into his own. Either way, it was a bit difficult for me to embrace. As a mother of two older daughters, I fully understood there would be a transition from elementary school to junior high, yet I was caught off guard by the changes that had appeared seemingly overnight in David.

It all came to light on the first day of seventh grade, when I told David I would walk him to our new bus stop. Living in the outer fringes of the Twin Cities, the designated stop is on a county road where the posted speed is 50 miles per hour. It was a perfect September morning, the early-morning dew still clinging to the tall grasses lining the ditch as the sun inched higher in the eastern sky.

"There's where you should wait," I instructed David, pointing toward the shoulder of the roadway. Since no other kids get on at our stop, I wanted to make sure he wasn't too close to the busy commuter traffic.

"Don't stand by me," he suddenly ordered.

"I'll wait here until we can see the bus."

"No, you can leave." His cheerful attitude from minutes earlier suddenly disappeared, and his eyebrows came together in a frown.

"I'll cross the street," I suggested.

"No—go home!"

I crossed the street and walked about a house-length away.

"Farther, Mom!" he called without looking at me.

"This is far enough," I insisted. "No one knows I'm waiting with you."

I recalled when I was in junior high how humiliating it was for my mother to show up at the school. My mother was forty-nine when I was born, so by the time I was in junior high, she was in her sixties, gray hair and all. Although my parents had retired from farming and moved to town, one could always expect to see my mother's well-rounded figure in old-fashioned kitchen dresses rather than the hip polyester styles of the times.

But I dress cool, I thought to myself, quickly

glancing at my trendy capris and T-shirt.

"Mom! Go home!" he shouted with urgency, the bus now approaching.

I started walking slowly up the street, sneaking a peek to make sure David got on safely, and then continued my morning walk, trying in earnest to make sense of this abrupt change.

What happened to our special bond? I wondered, thinking back to first grade, when David developed a huge crush on the cutest girl in his class, Laura. That first day when I picked him up from school, David insisted on following her so he could find out where she lived.

"I don't recognize her from the neighborhood, David," I said as he got in the car.

"Follow her, Mom. Quick—she's in the red van!"

"David, we can't follow her. We'll just wait for the new directory to come out."

"No! Hurry before you lose them," he insisted.

Giving in to his six-year-old innocence and big brown eyes, I tried following their van inconspicuously, to no avail. Heartbroken, David sat in the back seat, his bottom lip protruding in disappointment. Since I worked at the local police department, I knew how to get their address without stalking Laura and her mother.

I can't believe I'm doing this for a first-grade crush, I'd thought as I ran the plate number the next day in the state computer. I copied down the address, noting it was only a few blocks from our house, and that afternoon I proudly told my son. "Okay, David. I know exactly where Laura lives."

"Let's go!" he chimed, waving his hand forward, thrilled to simply drive by her house. David and Laura became good friends that year, but we always kept my detective work our little secret.

Continuing my morning walk, the paved sidewalk came to an end and I opted for a shortcut through a thick grove of trees. The uneven dirt path reminded me of the state park hiking trails and our tradition of three moms and three kids camping together one weekend each summer. Each year, David could hardly wait to get the tent set up so he could run off to explore the campground, planning our next adventure. But his favorite time came late at night, after the s'mores and campfires, for our quiet, sometimes whispered, mother-son talks in the tent.

As I made the last turn for home, I recalled the year he missed me so much at camp. The summer after fifth grade, David attended church camp with his best friend. It was his third year at the same camp, and he was quite familiar with the week-long program, so I hadn't expected him to be lonely. The camp is located a three-hour drive north of the Twin Cities, and even though they provide bus transportation, my friend and I enjoy driving the boys ourselves. Just as in previous years, we drove back on their last day to pick them up. As I entered the camp parking lot, I caught sight of two boys in dirty jean shorts and T-shirts, approaching my car, one at a very rapid pace.

Oh, that's David, I realized, through the layers of dirt. I waved and pulled into a parking spot. Instead of standing back and waiting for me to come to a stop, he took a running leap onto the side of the vehicle, clinging to the driver's door. Immediately, I applied the brake and jerked to a stop.

"David! Let me stop the car!" I said.

The second I opened the door, he wrapped his arms around me, tears springing to his eyes.

"What's the matter?" I asked, worried something was wrong.

"I j-just missed you sooo m-much!" he choked without releasing his grasp.

I held him tightly for several moments, surprised at his emotion.

So, understandably, this sudden distance he required at the bus stop was a little difficult for me to accept. I went on about my day, getting home from work shortly before David got off the bus. With the morning lesson still fresh in my mind, I simply waited for him well out of view, inside the house.

"How was the first day?" I inquired as he scrounged for an after-school snack.

"Great."

"Really?"

"Lots of girls," he clarified.

"So, everything went okay?"

"They knew you were my mom," he said with a hint of mortification. "It was a little obvious." He sighed, reiterating his point of the morning.

"Got it, bud."

Later that evening, I reminded David he was no longer on a carefree summer schedule and needed to get ready for bed. My husband and I went downstairs to his room and talked with him about junior high and homework expectations before saying good night and prayers. I then retreated upstairs to finish folding laundry, facing the reality that my son was maturing and needed some space.

Only a few minutes later, I noticed him in the kitchen.

"I thought you were in bed," I said.

"I was thirsty," he answered, heading toward the stairway with a glass of water. "Good night."

"Good night, bud," I said, resuming my folding.

Just then David called from the stairs. "Mom? Can you tuck me in again?"

A smile crossed my face, and I laid the clothes aside. "You bet I will."

Barbara Marshak

Love Is a Tractor

Prior to the birth of my son, Dylan, I knew a lot about children. I find that most childless people suffer from this delusion. "Just say no," I would spout. "Don't buy them this. Don't feed them that." Of course I was an expert. I wasn't a parent.

One particular phrase from my B. D. (Before Dylan) days that has come to bite me on the behind is, "If I ever have a son, I will encourage him to play with dolls." I was a strong supporter of the theory that nurture can trump nature. "He can have the odd car or two, but he is also going to have dolls and tea sets, to balance things out," I would pontificate. I equated raising a boy who would one day become a loving and tender husband and father with knowing how to host a tea party. And, if I had no daughters, I would still have someone to play house with.

Well, here I am, with a testosterone-fueled two-year-old, and the phrase "boys will be boys" now rings true. Instead of gentle pats on my cheek, I get sideswiped by his fire engine. Bites are kisses. And head butting, like "aloha," translates into both hello and goodbye. I spend most of my days trying to avoid being wrestled to the floor.

Oh, I tried to instill some decorum. "Nicely! Gently!" I used to yell at the top of my lungs as my little angel mauled Grandma in the name of love.

There are a few things, however, that receive Dylan's gentle touch. What does he cherish? The very icons of manhood—his 1,001 cars, trucks, planes, trains, boats, and tractors. Plastic and die-cast replicas of everything from Model Ts to space shuttles blanket the kitchen, right through the living room and on up the stairs and into his bedroom.

We never did buy a tea set.

The one dolly he did have, although he never gave it any attention, mysteriously disappeared on an excursion with Dad. His father seems to relish the fact that his son is "all boy."

I am not blind to the irony of the situation. I have relinquished my dream of being his guest at high tea. I have been sucked into his world of emergency vehicles and John Deere farming equipment. I indulge his need, obviously biological, to create construction sites in the sandbox and to have impromptu car races in the kitchen.

Each night he tucks a car under each arm and toddles off to bed—no doubt to dream of monster wrecking machines, junkyards, and racetracks, where he can drive (*vrooomm–vroommm*) to his heart's delight. We have witnessed him in his car bed, sound asleep, with his small hands steering an invisible wheel.

I can envision it now: He is sixteen, in the garage, psyched over a barely roadworthy coup. Car parts litter the garage floor, oil is smeared on his Nascar T-shirt, and I'm telling the girls who keep calling that he is in his room, composing sonnets.

I try not to ruminate about the course we might be headed on: Video games instead of Monopoly or Scrabble. Comic books in lieu of the classics. Farting, burping, and slurping instead of "please," "thank you," and "excuse me." Stinky, funky socks underneath the sofa. Rotting bananas forgotten in knapsacks. Multi-legged critters living in desk drawers. Grime-encrusted sinks and bathtubs.

But the other night I caught a glimpse of what kind of man he will be. When I was tucking him into bed, he handed me his prized possession, a green die-cast tractor.

"Lub you," my little auto aficionado said before turning on his side.

So, perhaps I will, after all, send a young man into the world who is generous and loving. And if he can manage to pop his head out from underneath the hood of his latest junker, the rest of the world just might see it, too.

Tracy L. Doerr

A version of "Love Is a Tractor" was first published in *Big Apple Parent*, April 2004.

Sediment of the Past

A friend recently asked me why she had never heard me mention my mother. The question surprised me, for my mother has been dead more than twenty years and few people have asked me about her. Perhaps they intuited a wound I have never been able to cauterize and so steered clear of it.

I was sixteen when my mother died, and I was just beginning to understand that she was more than my mother, that she was a strong woman who believed in substance more than style, integrity more than money, and forthrightness more than charm. She was the woman who shaped my childhood and early adolescence. Her influence runs deeper than the genes I inherited from her. The core of who I am, full of contradictions and complexities, whispers her name incessantly, every day. Although she is dead, she remains alive within me.

She taught me to drive by coaxing me to chauffeur her around town in her Chevy Vega. I did my best to feign teenage nonchalance while she did the real work of telling me when to depress the clutch and guiding my hand through the four gears.

I remember the warmth of her touch and the sensitivity that resonated in her voice. I remember her dark hair and eyes and the way she looked intently at me whenever I disappointed her. When I was in fifth grade, the principal sent me home for fighting, and I could hardly face her. She didn't need to say anything. Her eyes told me how deeply my mercurial temper had wounded her.

My mother had cancer of the lymphatic system, but she never told me, and I don't recall her being ill. One day she went to the hospital, and a few days later she died. Her death was so sudden that I never got to ask my mother, the woman who had been my confidant, why she hadn't told me of her illness. I never told her how deeply I love her, and I cannot now tell her how much I miss her. Nothing I ever do can restore her to me, this woman who had been at the core of my life for sixteen years.

My friend's question conjured up this complex battery of memories and emotions. For an instant, I was again a child, and my mother was lulling me to sleep by reading me a little book about faraway lands. The moment gone, I felt terribly uncomfortable and found myself unable to answer my friend's question. I could manage only to say that I hadn't seen my mother in a long time.

Her question awakened in me the fear that someday Francesca, my four-year-old daughter, will ask about my mother—her grandmother. She must be dimly aware that she knows both maternal grandparents but only her paternal grandfather. What will I tell her when she corners me? Perhaps I'll say that her grandmother would have liked more than anything to have cradled her when she was born, as she had cradled me, that she would have wanted to see her learn to walk, and that she would have loved her as much as she loved me. These words may demand more courage than I have.

This truth is, I want to preserve Francesca's innocence, her belief that all is right. I never want her to know that children in Rwanda, the Sudan, and countless other places grow up without any family and with the conviction that violence is the norm. I want to shield her from the fact that we inhabit a world in which tyrants maintain power by butchering people and speaking hateful words. I don't want Francesca to learn that she can never know her paternal grandmother in the intimate way I knew her. But I can't insulate her from the world any more than I can make my mother live again.

At best, I can try to hold on to the sediment of

the past, while helping Francesca move toward the future. The past and future will intersect when she comes to me with the desire that her grandmother be as vivid to her as she is to me. Together, Francesca and I will excavate the memories and emotions that are my childhood, and she will come to know her grandmother as she comes to understand herself.

Already, I see traces of my mother in Francesca, this girl so gentle and so earnest. She has my mother's eyes, dark and intense, with a premonition of passion yet to awaken. She speaks with a hint of my mother's tone and cadence: quick, full of energy, and always searching to understand, rather than to judge. Francesca has a genuine and effortless warmth that draws people to her. It is the same warmth I knew as a child.

This spring, Francesca helped me plant peas and potatoes in our garden. With a hoe, I etched furrows in the soil, and close beside me she lined them with peas and potato eyes. She did this work with a precision and seriousness that one might have thought impossible for a four-year-old. In her tiny leather boots and Minnie Mouse shirt, she was a cross between a gardener and an elf. Her grandmother would have been proud of her.

Christopher Cumo

Take Me Out to the Ball Game

I wasn't born loving baseball, but I believe my son Jack was. His four siblings have all played the game, but the older three discouraged him when he expressed his desire to play baseball. "Too slow, too long, too boring," came the refrain from the sister and brothers, who eventually turned to soccer, wrestling, and basketball. His little brother just kind of ran the other way when Jack appeared with a bat and ball. I've heard stories, though, that my father, who died when I was very young, had a great talent for the sport. I like to believe that some of his spirit and love of baseball live on in Jack . . . and in me.

When Jack was five, amidst protests of "I want to play baseball," we signed him up for a town soccer league. He had always been quite a handful, extremely rambunctious and active, and he had difficulty remembering what he was taught. Through testing, we had recently discovered he had learning disabilities, the most challenging of which was attention deficit disorder with hyperactivity. Soccer seemed like a perfect way to channel his boundless energy—except Jack wanted to play baseball.

That same summer, a group of my family members decided to take in a Minor League baseball game. We live in the Buffalo, New York, area, home to the Buffalo Bisons, the AAA team of the Cleveland Indians. My husband and I planned to attend the game with Jack. When my husband got sick at the last minute, I rather grudgingly took Jack myself. This would be a long night.

We took our seats out by left field, but Jack kept insisting we had to move closer. After a couple innings, in order to appease him, we left our group and found some empty seats above the third base dugout. There, the same little boy who couldn't sit through a Disney movie or complete his assignments in school sat through nine innings of baseball. He remembered the final score for months. That Bison's baseball game became a defining moment in his life and also in our relationship. We became "baseball buddies."

The following summer Jack played baseball. Not only was he attentive to his own position, I often observed him giving instruction out on the field to the other six- and seven-year-olds . . . on both teams. Cartoons were replaced by *Sports Center*.

While Jack has become a loyal follower of all Buffalo teams, baseball remains his passion. Somewhere along the way, he also became a steadfast Yankee fan and swept me in with him. Jack, like many boys, dreams of holding a position on that fabled team. He sleeps in a room surrounded by the Yankee logo, pennants, and legends, past and present. The Babe greets you at the door, and Jeter, Williams, and Wells look down at you from places of honor shared with the smiling images of Maris and Mantle.

A few years into Jack's Little League career, we made the ninety-mile drive to Toronto with his dad and younger brother, Ethan, to watch the Yankees beat the Blue Jays. We eventually saw the Yankees play in Cleveland and Baltimore.

One year Jack begged us, "I want to go where the Yankee fans are. I want to go to the Bronx."

Going to a game at Yankee Stadium, though only seven hours away by car, had somehow seemed unattainable before. All it took was Jack's persistence and online ticketing, and we found ourselves in that most sacred of ball parks—the house that Ruth built.

When he was eleven, Jack's solid performance on the ball field led him to be chosen for a travel team that would culminate with a week of play in Cooperstown, New York, home of the National Baseball Hall of Fame and Museum. But just before he turned twelve, he stopped hitting the ball and the coaches informed us Jack wasn't playing up to their expectations. Sadly, my husband and I decided to take him off the travel team.

Despite feeling disappointed that he didn't get to Cooperstown, Jack continued to play on the town league. That, along with much pitching from his dad, a lot of time spent in batting cages, and his pure tenacity brought him to tryouts for his middle school team the next spring. After making it through two weeks and three cuts, he was once again disappointed when he didn't make the school's team.

He was also having a hard time academically. By the end of sixth grade, he had worked himself out of all special assistance for his learning disabilities. Middle school left him struggling to maintain passing grades in some subjects. Still, he persevered and made it through.

Jack will begin high school next fall. Life, including baseball, continually challenges my son and tests his endurance. While studies have always come easily to his sister and brothers, Jack rarely questions why he has to work so much harder. His resilience, determination, and ability to hang in there when others would become discouraged continue to amaze me.

It is especially in baseball, though, that I most see his unwavering spirit. Whether he's bouncing balls off his pitch-back or diving to catch the popup near second base, Jack's drive and enthusiasm are contagious. Every day is game seven of the World Series.

Though it is usually father and son who bond with sports, it is my son and I who share a special place in our hearts for baseball. Sure, Dad is the one who hits balls and plays catch with him. But I'm the one who, along with Jack, insists that we arrive "very early" for batting practice and who buys tickets to games. A few years back, after his younger brother's growing rebellion to bow out of our annual Yankee/Blue Jay trek to Toronto, Jack and I decided to head up there on our own. This continues to be a mother-son tradition I wouldn't give up for the world.

Last summer, Jack's town league team was undefeated. Determined to make the school team in the spring, he hit balls at indoor facilities through the long Buffalo winter and played catch with his father even when there was a foot of snow on the ground. When the time for tryouts finally arrived, my anxiety level was sky-high, despite everyone constantly reminding me that it was "just baseball." I even said a prayer to God, and one to my father, that maybe those angels in the outfield could lend a hand. The day he walked up to my car after school and announced, "I'm on the team," I thought my heart would burst.

Not long ago, I found a crumpled up essay that had fallen out of Jack's backpack. It was about me. Smiling, I read words every mother loves to hear—that my son recognizes and appreciates how much I help him in school and "in life." But it was the next part that brought the tears:

> My mom and I like baseball. She is the one who has taken me to lots of my baseball practices. When I have games, she always cheers me on, even if I am playing horribly. My mom was the one who got me tickets to my first Yankees game.

I don't know how anyone can say, "It's just baseball." It is so much more. It's sharing the hopes and dreams that someday he'll be the next Derek Jeter. It's eating hot dogs together and watching a double play or hearing the strains from "The Natural" as a ball sails over the fence on a perfect summer night. It's getting off the Number Four train with a boy who will never forget his first trip to Yankee Stadium.

JoEllen Murphy

The Pediatrician Visit

U nless there is a shot to be given or blood to be drawn, a trip to the pediatrician usually is uneventful once you get past those nerve-wracking monthly visits of the first year. Barring the exceptional stitches from a soccer game or a new pair of rollerblades and the occasional croupy cough and spiked fevers, a typical visit to the pediatrician seems rather commonplace.

Until adolescence.

When adolescence hits, it's a whole different ball game. Visits to the pediatrician become complicated and demand an entirely new set of rules. Especially if you have a son. Every mother of a son should know this truth: The day will come when it is time to step out of the examining room and let your boy fend for himself. They don't talk about this in baby books or on the Discovery channel; no one ever warns you it's going to happen or prepares you for it. You can rely only on your instincts to tell you when it's time to step back into the waiting room and stay there, Mom.

I learned the hard way.

Last year when our son, Matt, was twelve, his glands became swollen and I took him to see the doctor. His regular pediatrician was on vacation, so we saw Dr. Earl, who performs musical comedies at the local community theater.

I was explaining Matt's symptoms when suddenly, before I could even finish, Dr. Earl held up his hand to stop me and smiled. I thought he was about to break into a song.

"I know exactly the problem," he announced. "Adolescence!" Then he proceeded to pull back Matt's waistband on his boxer shorts and look beyond.

My son's eyes widened in terror.

I didn't know what to do. Should I leave? Should I bolt for the door? Too late.

Dr. Earl began to describe more than I ever needed to know about my son's current anatomy: size, shape, you get the picture . . . and so, unfortunately, did I. It was a toss-up as to which of us was more embarrassed: Matt or I. Dr. Earl seemed perfectly at ease.

"This is quite common in adolescence," he informed us, as if addressing a room filled with Harvard medical students instead of a shell-shocked twelve-year-old and his hyperventilating middle-aged mom. "Once the testosterone kicks in, there's a surge of progesterone and that can cause swelling and tenderness around the mammary glands. Some guys actually develop breasts."

I wondered if I needed smelling salts. For Matt. Not for me. It's bad enough for a pubescent guy to hear all of this. But to have your mother hear it, too?

It must be terrifying for Matt. His body is changing so quickly from day to day, and he has absolutely no control over it. His clothes don't fit him anymore, and his voice is getting deeper and sometimes cracks. The baby fat is melting away, and his face doesn't look like a little boy's anymore. No wonder he swaggers and acts like he's such a tough guy, cussing and spitting with his buddies. He must be panicked. The body he's been living in is taking on a whole new life of its own. He looks different. He smells different. No wonder he acts different, pulling away and not sharing with us the way he used to. If I'm having trouble seeing the Matt I've always known in the face and body of this much-changed version of our son, I'm sure Matt must be having the same trouble, too.

After we left the office, Matt didn't want to talk about the doctor's visit. He slipped the earphones of his Walkman on as soon as we climbed into the car, and he was incommunicado for the long drive home.

"Did that weird you out?" I asked him later, when he was finally willing to let the world in again.

"Duh, yeah!"

"You're not going to grow breasts," I assured him. "It's just a hormone—progesterone. Pregnant women get it."

"Thanks, Mom," he said sarcastically, as I realized I wasn't helping by comparing him to a pregnant lady.

For the first time as his mother, I felt powerless to help my son. For twelve years, I had watched him grow—from that first black-and-white image in the sonogram to the size 10 Nike-filling, growing man in front of me now. I had chartered and known his every change. From his first tooth to the first freckles on his face. I'd seen his hair change colors, grow dark and strong with age, and lose its blond baby silkiness. I'd watched his compact little boy's body stretch out, and his muscles form from his first August of tackle football.

At twelve, a son grows in front of his mother, but it's not for her to chart the changes anymore, like writing in the baby book—how many pounds he's gained, how many inches he's grown. His body is growing in ways that only he can chart now and that I will never know. When he was a baby, I was his whole life. My breasts gave him nourishment; my hands changed his diapers. My lips kissed his tears and his boo-boos; my arms held and protected him from the world. He used to fall asleep to my singing, and my words became his words as he learned and copied and mimicked.

My ears heard his every sound, and my whole body responded to whatever he needed.

I used to cuddle with Matt on the couch when he was little—but no more. He always used to take my hand when we crossed the street together, but he stopped doing that several years ago. Sometimes, his fingers still touch mine if we're somewhere new. A brief brush of fingers, and he'll take my hand for only a second. As if telling me, "I'm still here, Mom." Deep inside the bravado and swagger is the little boy who remains. I miss seeing him and having him around all the time. But I can't wait to meet the man he is becoming.

Darlene Craviotto

 Outside the Box

We got married on Valentine's Day. Twenty-two years later, on Independence Day, he walked out. Holidays are big in our house.

We had moved into the house with a twenty-one-month-old baby boy, and precisely one month later, our second son was born. Now, my teenage sons and I lived alone in the house, and the first postdivorce Christmas was looming. For the first time ever, the boys would wake up on Christmas morning with just one parent, me, their mom. My heart was broken. My dreams of a fairy-tale marriage were shattered. And I just knew that some emotion would blindside me right when the boys needed smiles.

But, wait. What about breaking out of the box altogether? No decorations, no Christmas presents under a tree, no tree, no stockings, and no possibility of snow.

I approach the boys. "Hey, guys. What if we went to the Bahamas on a cruise over Christmas? Would that be okay?"

Sons: "Whooey! Naked women!"

"No, no naked women. This will be a family cruise, and we'll have to share a cabin, but we can roam all over the ship any hour of the day."

Sons: "Whooey! Teenage girls in bikinis. Karaoke at midnight. Drinking."

"No, no drinking. You're too young. But when we dock at the ports, like Saint Thomas, you can play Frisbee on the white sandy beaches and swim in turquoise-colored seawater, and you'll meet lots of new friends."

Sons: "Yeah! Let's go!"

"But," I ask tentatively, "what about not seeing your dad on Christmas?"

Sons: "That's okay, Mom. He'll be fine."

So, I book it, charge it, and five days before Christmas, we're airborne. The challenge of this journey will be for me to get some sea legs—both on board and emotionally.

My sons are like two sides of the same coin, nearly inseparable. While one is wild, the other thinks. While one smiles charmingly, the other flirts outrageously. One is tall, dark, and moves languidly; the other is muscular, chic, and likely to do flips at the least provocation. They're entertaining, and they buoy my spirits as we undertake the seemingly endless flight from the Pacific Northwest to Miami, Florida.

Once on board, the families sprawl throughout the cruise ship. Most feature not only both parents, but also cousins, aunts, uncles, and grandparents; all are present. It's just the three of us. Mother and sons. I feel like a four-legged chair with one leg missing.

Exhaustion rolls over me, and I say, half in jest, "I hope that by the end of this journey, I look twenty years younger."

There are endless lines on the ship. I send one son or the other to see what's at the head of the line. Several times, they return to tell me and say, "Someone stopped, and everyone just lined up behind him." That's the odd psychology of cruise ships.

We spend a lot of time together, my sons and I. We dress up for dinner, and we chat and laugh and sing with the waiters. We find pieces of ourselves hidden in the smiles of strangers, and we pull out yards of conversation where, before, at home, there were hugs, yes, and "I love you" often said, but no stories. Here, thousands of miles from home, being rocked to sleep by gentle waves and awakened by the power blast of the sun, we are full of stories.

My boys reveal that they are thrilled that, finally, I have friends, male and female, instead of just burying my heart and soul in interviewing authors, producing the audio for a couple of national shows, and anchoring the news. I learn that they are proud of me for doing the right thing, the right way. They are happier, they say, that Dad gets to be Dad and Mom gets to be Mom—and they get to live with me.

They sternly warn me about guys. "They're after only one thing, Mom."

No problem on this ship. The only single guy is the headliner, a comedian who labels me "hot mama" and invites me to coffee. Which—remembering my sons' words—is just what he gets.

Christmas Day, we dock in Saint Thomas, and they take me to a jewelry store. My teenage sons buy me diamond drop earrings that I still wear every day and that they're still paying for. The few gifts we exchange are in brilliant contrast to the piles of gifts under the tree in Christmases past. I treasure this gift, from sons who are now young men.

In the sunshine and gentled by the sea breeze, we suddenly stand taller, walk with a spirited tempo, laugh more easily, and, in opening to other families, find freedom in our own family. I meet their on-board friends, a group of five kids, then ten, then twenty, and then their friends' parents.

One day, when we're tanned and well fed and full of joy, it is time to step off the ship. As we gather our bags and move off the ship, a security man checking identifications turns to me.

"These are your *sons*? No way. This is *your* ID? You

look twenty years younger."

I just smiled. Then the three of us—my sons and I—sailed off the ship, feeling as balanced as a three-legged stool. Mother and sons.

Less than a week later, back home, after our untraditional Christmas full of unexpected gifts, there's a knock on the door. A boy from the cruise stands on the front porch, wanting to stay for a while. We embrace him. When he leaves, another boy—a local, longtime friend of my sons—arrives, and, he, too, lives with us for a while. Suddenly, I am a mom with many sons and a heart bursting with joy. And I've got my sea legs now.

Diana Jordan

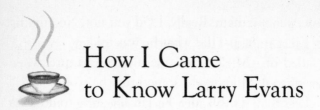

How I Came to Know Larry Evans

Mr. Evans came into my home, completely unannounced and uninvited, in 1996, the year my son, Mike, was a ninth grader at DCTS, Dauphin County Technical School. Suddenly, my son, my precious child, who, until that time, had never given me a bit of grief, started announcing he didn't have to do anything he didn't want to do. Mr. Evans had said so.

My initial reaction was, "Oh, yeah? Ya wanna bet on that, buddy?"

At the dinner table almost every night, my husband and I heard the same refrains: "Mr. Evans said this." "Mr. Evans said that." "Mr. Evans did this." "Mr. Evans did that." We were beginning to wonder about this Mr. Evans. What was this man trying to do to our son and to our relationship with our son?

Here was a boy who, when told what his chores

were, just did them. Really, I kid you not. No arguing, no stalling, he just did what he was told.

But after Mr. Evans came into the picture, when I would ask Mike to do something, he would say, "I don't have to do this for you. I'm choosing to do it for you because I want to."

Well, okay, I thought, *as long as it gets done, I won't argue with why you are doing it.*

We live on a farm; there is a lot to get done. Still, I was concerned about this "I only have to do what I want to do" concept. That is not the way the world works; there are things you just have to do, like it or not.

So, not too long into Mike's newfound "self-determination," I decided I'd better talk to my fifteen-year-old and explain that life is not that simple. Besides, Dad and Grandpa were not taking his "doing them a favor" attitude too well when hay from the barn needed to be stacked on a buyer's truck. They were both getting a little irritated.

I headed to Mike's bedroom, got comfortable on his bed while he played video baseball, and asked, "What's up with this?"

He laughed and said he'd been waiting for me to ask.

He went into animated detail about the personal and social responsibility class he was taking at DCTS. Mr. Evans, of course, was the teacher. Mike talked excitedly about what he was learning. He explained that the only things in life over which you have no

choice are birth and death, that absolutely everything
else is a choice. So, you have to weigh your options to
make the right choices.

"For instance," he said, "you can choose not to pay
your taxes, but in doing so, you have chosen to go to
jail or at least pay a hefty fine."

One of his favorite examples of this choice process
was a story in the class material about a Jewish man
who had been in a concentration camp during the
Holocaust. This man's story was horrible, but amazing.
Mike told me how the man had been surrounded by
evil. Death and dying were everyday events; hunger
and humiliation were constant companions. Yet, the
man held his head high, choosing each day not only
to live with dignity and self-respect, but also to treat
others with dignity and respect—even his captors.

"The Nazis could take everything from him," Mike
went on. "They could strip him naked, take all his
belongings, and murder his family, but they could not
take his soul. He would not allow them to steal his
dignity as a human being. Who he was and who he
would remain were his choices, not theirs."

Mike was so impressed by the man's story; I was,
too. I was also impressed with how deeply my son
was thinking all this through, and I was intrigued by
what he was learning. Mr. Evans obviously was not
the enemy we'd at first thought him to be.

Toward the end of Mike's class with Mr. Evans, he

told me the class was being offered as a night course for parents. Mike really wanted me to go to the class. I tried to explain that, with working full-time outside the home, raising two kids, and helping with the family farm, well, I just had no time for a class. Mike insisted. He offered to help me make the time to go; he would take care of his little sister and take over many of my chores.

He kept his end of the deal, and so did I. For six weeks, I attended Mr. Evans's class.

As a customer relations representative, I have had the privilege of attending many very good courses in human relationships. None of them did for my family what Mr. Evans's personal and social responsibility class did. It opened up a line of communication that I doubt would have been possible otherwise. It taught me to see my child as a young adult on the threshold of manhood—and as an individual who was going to make his own choices, good or bad.

The class taught me that I could not be in control of or responsible for everything my child did. I came to understand and accept that Mike would be making more and more of his own decisions and that he would live with the consequences of those decisions. The course helped Mike and me—and, by association, my husband—to work toward a relationship of mutual respect, toward a friendship and a love that could maintain us for a lifetime together, as adults.

It is never easy for any parent when a child begins to cut the parental ties, demanding in word and action their own space on this planet. Learning to respect their right to independence from you is a hard, hard thing to grasp.

In the next few years after Mr. Evans's class, Mike did make many decisions for himself, most good and a few bad. What Mike gained from his time with Mr. Evans was not freedom to do as he pleased. There were still rules that had to be followed in our home and consequences for rules broken. What Mike did gain was wisdom as to why those rules were in place to begin with and the knowledge that ultimately it was his choice whether he lived in peace with his family, his school, his peers, and his society. Mike usually chose to walk in peace.

The most important thing Mike gained from his class with Mr. Evans was a better relationship with his parents during his teenage years. Instead of having parents who tried to control every move he made at a time in his life when holding on tighter seemed like the right thing to do, we learned to hold on loosely, but never let go.

Mike is gone now. He died the first week of his senior year at DCTS. Yes, as with most teenage deaths, it was the result of a very bad choice.

Do I regret giving Mike the freedom to choose his path? No. I have very few regrets where Mike is concerned.

Fortunately, I learned how to deal with my teenager without the typical huge fights, without the anger and tears. Because of the lessons we learned, we came to know each other in a way that would have taken years into his adulthood. We did not have those years to mend the bridges that tend to get burned during the tumultuous teenage years. Thankfully, there were no bridges to mend—we didn't burn our bridges; we reinforced them.

I don't know whether when you die is, ultimately, a choice, too. My husband tends to think that if Mike had not chosen to get into that car on that morning, he would still be alive. I believe that the day you are born and the day you die are set in stone; that how you live your life is where the choices lie. It doesn't matter which one of us is right; we're probably both wrong. What does matter is how you leave the people you've loved. Have you left them better for knowing you?

The last day of Mr. Evans's class is called "Uncle Laird Day." You are to imagine it is your last day on Earth, that at the end of today, you will die. The assignment is to write letters to the most important people in your life, telling them what they have meant to you and what you hope you've meant to them.

A few months ago, I came across the letters I wrote that day. The letter to my daughter was very touching, filled with love for my little girl, my hopes for her life, my sadness that I would not meet her children but my confidence that she would be a wonderful mom. Reading those words of love for her and regret for missing her future tugged at my heart.

But it was my letter to Mike that stopped me in my tracks.

There was no talk of his future children, even though I had always believed he would be a really good dad. There was no talk of his career plans or the paths that lay ahead of him. The letter I wrote to Mike was about us, about him and me, about how much I loved him, that his soul was a huge part of my soul, and that, no matter where in the vast realm of this universe we meet again, I will know him instantly.

I explained to him how much I would miss the intimate friendship we shared and how thankful I was that we had that kind of a relationship. I told him to be intuitive and that, if there were any way for souls to communicate after death, his and mine would be the ones to do it. I said that, because we had learned how to reach each other so well on Earth, we would probably be able to reach beyond the veil of death, if it was allowed.

I can tell you, it is allowed, and Mike has reached me, many times and in many ways. But that is a story for another time. For now, I will leave you with the lessons learned:

Love your children well. They are a gift. They

are not your creation or possession. They are souls passing this way but once, just as you are. Work on a relationship that will bless you both now and give the one left behind, whether that be parent or child, something to hold until you meet again.

Yes, how we live and how we love are definitely choices that carry profound consequences.

Thank you, Mr. Evans, for coming into my home unannounced and uninvited. You are welcome here anytime.

Shari Bowes Deaven

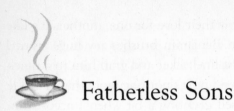# Fatherless Sons

As my son, Benjamin, and I wait to board our plane at the San Francisco airport, I find myself staring at a teenage boy and his father in line ahead of us. About fourteen, the boy wears surfer shorts that reach below his knees, and his spiky dark-blond hair is sun-streaked. I think of my boys, who looked so much like little surfers when we took them to Hawaii and they glided on their boogie boards at the ocean's edge. Little tanned, blond boys with sun-whitened hair, just like mine used to be every summer. I stroke my eight-year-old's hair for a second—he's immersed in his Harry Potter book—but I don't take my eyes off the teenager.

He raises his head from his computer game and says something to his father. The man rests his arm on his son's shoulder and squeezes briefly, then turns it into a playful jostle, as if remembering how men are supposed to show their love for one another. It's like what I do when Benjamin brushes my hugs away. I charge him like a linebacker and grab him in a quick, rough hug, pretending it's nothing more than a tackle. I even find myself grunting a bit when I accost him, my voice deepening in a male-bonding kind of way.

It isn't until the man smiles at his son that I see their resemblance. The man is balding, and his eyes are a different shape than his son's, but when they smile at each other, there's no question they are father and son. Their lips, teeth, and the crease appearing in their chins when they smile are identical. I'll be embarrassed if they turn and catch me intruding on this private moment, but I'm riveted.

When I catch a glimpse of my face in store windows now, I see my mother. I've always had her long, stalky body and eyes that disappear when we smile, but now, at forty-three, my whole face is becoming hers. Even our lips, pressed into thin lines when we're concentrating—or masking our feelings—are identical.

If women turn into their mothers at a certain age, do men turn into their fathers? My sons share many of my physical characteristics, but how much do they resemble the sperm donor, their biological father? Six-year-old Thomas inherited my family's dark smudges under his eyes, but I don't recognize Benjamin's mini–Captain Spock eyebrows. Did these come from the man we don't know? This might be important to him when he reaches adolescence—when he tries to figure out who he is, where he belongs, and what man he came from.

When people ask about Benjamin's and Thomas's "dad" or "father," I hurry to correct them. "The donor," I say, because there is no dad in this family.

A few months earlier, Thomas and I walked home from the library together. "How do you feel about not having a dad?" I said, concentrating on holding my voice steady. Keep it light. No big deal. Make it sound like, "Did you feed the dog this morning?"

"Um—" Thomas paused to think. "Sometimes good and sometimes bad."

Uh-oh. Here we go. What would he say? That he felt alone and sad? Maybe by first grade having two moms was no longer the envy of his friends like it had been in preschool. Maybe it was no longer enough to make up for the absence of a father.

"Okay," I said, preparing myself. "What's the bad thing about not having a dad?"

"Well, the bad is because you can climb up on a dad and he can lift you really high."

I wanted to laugh with relief. "You mean like Uncle does?"

"Yeah. I can touch the ceiling when he lifts me."

"Okay." I got ready for the rest. "What else?"

"That's all."

That's all? The only bad thing about not having

a dad is that there's no one to climb on? I wanted to believe him, to ease my worry, but I no longer assume he's telling me everything. He's old enough to know what might hurt my feelings, and he may be holding back to protect me.

Another lesbian mom debated with me at lunch once. "Don't you sometimes worry," she whispered across the table at a seafood restaurant, "that we're making our kids suffer because they don't have a father?"

I remembered a documentary on PBS called *That's a Family*, about families with divorce, adoption, foster parents, grandparents, or gay parents. When a twelve-year-old boy being raised by his single mother casually stated, "I don't have a dad," Benjamin turned to Pam and me and smiled. "That's like us." He looked pleased, not anguished.

"No," I said to the other mother. "I really don't."

I was insulted. How could she suggest that I'm not good enough? That I can't give them all they need, make up for the absence of a father?

"Benjamin and Thomas have never seemed upset," I told her. "They've never complained."

I thought of other reasons one could grow up without a father—death, divorce, abandonment. And about my friend, a widow whose son's bride-to-be told her, "Men raised by women are the best."

The other mother at the restaurant shook her

head, but I was so sure that day.

How can you grieve something you never lost? My sons have two parents, one biological and one adoptive, both of whom they've always known. They didn't lose a father. They were never abandoned. But now I know I'm just too close to it. Just because my sons don't tell me it bothers them doesn't mean that's the case. And things might change as they get older.

"Well, what about the good?" I asked Thomas, as we turned the corner on our block. "What's good about not having a dad?"

"It's good because they're meaner. Jack told me his dad is meaner than his mom."

All right. Score another for the two moms.

"You're like the dad."

I almost stumbled on the sidewalk. "I'm like the dad?"

"Yeah, you're meaner than Mama."

I laughed but wanted to cry. I knew he meant "stricter" when he said "mean," and he's got me pegged. I am the heavy. If I think Pam's being walked over, I'm there handing out more severe consequences. I shout more, and louder. Even same-sex parents must fall into the good cop/bad cop roles.

"But you know I love you, right?" I asked.

It was lame, but I was desperate. It hurt to be called the mean mom. I wanted to be known as the mom who lets him wrap his arms and legs around me like a baby monkey and who kisses the warm spot in the crook of his neck. The mom who plays basketball in the driveway and pitches baseballs at the park. Who cheers her voice raw from the sidelines of the soccer field. The mom who wakes him up with kisses and a back rub and combs his silky bangs away from his face with her fingers. Does he appreciate any of this?

"Yeah, I know," he said, glancing up at me and grinning. "You love me."

I'm saved.

"But you're still meaner."

If my children, when they turn eighteen, do decide to locate their biological father, if they feel they lack a piece of their identity and need to find the man whose genes they share, or if they're just curious what he looks like, the sperm bank will furnish his name and address. I'd love to see a photo of the donor and maybe meet him, but I'll follow my boys' lead. I wonder if we'll ever run into any of the boys' half siblings; the donors are allowed a maximum of ten offspring. Will they want to find them also? I picture a family reunion with everyone wearing red T-shirts with the same inscription: "Family Reunion of Donor # 042-75."

Suddenly, a woman in the airport line immediately behind the boy and his father shifts her weight, and they notice her. The man says something to her, and she hands him a plane ticket. It takes me a moment to realize she is the boy's mother; she has been invisible, standing in this line behind them. This could be me in a few years: redundant, unnecessary now that the need for Mommy is less passionate, when I'm no longer the center of my sons' universe. So I see that this day comes for all mothers of sons. The time when we step aside, let them discover themselves as men, and wait for them to return. And, if we've done the best we could, they will. Without a doubt, I know they will.

Kathy Briccetti

Me in the Middle

As soon as I finished reading the invitation, I picked up the telephone and called my mother.

"I don't understand," I said.

"I'm adopting a Chinese doll as my daughter. Her name is Xue Ji, and we have invited you and your family to attend the official adoption ceremony."

"A doll?" I was more confused than ever.

Mom laughed. "At my age, a real toddler would require too much effort. Once I adopt Xue Ji, however, your daughter will no longer be the only adopted Chinese girl in the family."

Now, the invitation began to make sense, or at least as much sense as I could expect from the original thinker who had raised me. I smiled, even though I knew my mother couldn't see my expression. "That is very kind of you."

"Kind, shmind. It will be fun. My friends are all excited."

I winced. "Your friends?" How far had the madness spread?

"Betty—she's the seamstress—is making Xue Ji a wardrobe of traditional Chinese clothes. Mary is organizing the decorations. Karen is head chef; she's in charge of the kitchen."

"I assume we'll be eating Chinese."

"Of course. Karen even bought a new rice steamer. She already has several books about cooking Chinese dishes. Recipes are a hobby with her. She reads them for enjoyment."

My mother and her friends had been together since before I was born.

"What would you like us to do?" I asked.

"You and your wife are responsible for bringing your daughter to the event. Your daughter will play the part of the Chinese adoption authorities. She gets to stamp all the paperwork. There will be quite a lot."

"I remember the process as if it was yesterday." Most of the trip to China had been captured on videotape and absorbed by my mother soon after our return.

There was a brief pause on the other end of the line. "Be honest. Do you think I'm crazy?"

"Yes. But you're also doing a wonderful thing."

"Posh. Just don't be late."

Three days later, we entered my mother's house to find it transformed. Chinese lanterns hung from the ceiling. Chinese dragons danced across the walls. Every flat surface was topped with miniature Buddhas and other Chinese figurines. Chinese music was coming from the speakers, and the smells emanating from the kitchen transported me back to the country that had produced my daughter and entrusted my wife and I with her care.

My mother and her friends wore Chinese silk blouses.

My daughter was wide-eyed.

I was close to tears.

While a cynic might maintain that my mother wasn't doing anything she didn't want to, I knew the project was born of love. She wanted me to be happy, and that feeling extended to my family, to my daughter, in particular.

I kissed my mother and gave her a tight hug. "You've done a wonderful job here, Mom. For a moment I thought I'd just completed the fourteen-hour flight again."

"Perhaps you have."

My mother and her friends showed us around, pointing out their favorite touches and personal contributions, until we reached the doll sitting in a second high chair.

"This is Xue Ji."

I bowed. "Hello Xue Ji. We're pleased to meet you."

My daughter tugged at my pant leg. "Daddy, why are you talking to a doll? And why is she sitting at the table?"

"Your grandmother is adopting her. Just like your mother and I adopted you."

"But she's a doll."

I crouched. "*Shh.* Don't tell your grandmother. She thinks Xue Ji is a Chinese baby, like you."

My daughter stood tall. "I'm not a baby. I'm a kid."

"I know you're a kid. You're a big kid. Xue Ji will look up to you as if you were her older sister. She'll probably follow you around everywhere."

My daughter shook her head. "Dolls don't walk."

"We can pretend, just like when you play with your toys."

My daughter was not convinced, but she gave a little shrug anyway. "Okay. If that's what you want."

Mom clapped her hands together. "First, the adoption."

My mother led my daughter to her seat behind a children's desk and then went to retrieve Xue Ji.

"I would like to adopt this baby as my own."

Betty handed my daughter a stamp and ink pad. Mary laid a stack of documents on the desk. Karen was busily snapping photographs.

My daughter needed no further urging. She opened the ink pad and started stamping away, while my wife and I held hands and whispered about what a powerful experience this would probably prove. Our daughter was being given the chance to re-create an event that had been so pivotal to us all.

We had watched the tapes together, but my wife and I couldn't be certain how much our daughter really understood. After all, she watched puppets and cartoons on television, too.

This experience was physical and real.

Mom kissed my daughter on the top of her head and thanked her for her help. "Xue Ji is now my daughter."

Then the photography session began in earnest with every possible combination of participants captured for posterity.

My mother clapped a second time. "Let's eat to celebrate this magnificent event."

The food, as could be expected, was wonderful, a mixture of American Chinese and authentic Chinese cuisine. My daughter demonstrated her newly developed skill with chopsticks. The meal ended with fortune cookies, which must have been special ordered; each enclosed slip of paper read, "A child from China is a joy forever."

My mother leaned across the table and winked. "You're not so bad yourself."

I raised my cup of tea in salute. "I have only my mother to thank."

"Yes," she laughed, "you do."

The picture from that day my wife chose to frame and hang in our living room is a group shot. My daughter is sitting on my left, my mother is on my right, Xue Ji is propped up in front of me, and my wife is standing behind. That's me in the middle, surrounded by love.

Stephen D. Rogers

Roses and Rodents and Mom, Oh Yeah!

From the time my son, Sanford, could speak, he had the maturity of a person far beyond his years. By the time he was four or five, I usually treated Sandy more like a young adult than a child. I carefully explained circumstances and reasons for any rules or changes in our lives. I never acted dictatorially. Rarely did I have to correct him or punish him. We also shared many of the same interests, and he instinctively followed my train of thought, most of the time.

When Sandy was about six years old, a stranger sitting near us in a fast-food restaurant said, "Excuse me, but is that your son?"

"Yes," I answered, wondering why someone would ask the obvious.

"But you don't treat him like a child. You talk to him like he's your friend or something."

I turned back to the miniature guy sitting across

from me, his little feet swinging from the bench. "Oh," I said. "Well, he is my friend."

Before that conversation, I hadn't realized my son and I had such a mature relationship. Fortunately, our closeness continued, even through difficult times.

A year later, for example, my husband lost his job. My meager part-time income barely held us above water for the few months before he finally received an offer in another city. We scraped together our last few dollars and borrowed a few, as well, to pay for the move.

As soon as I'd unpacked our belongings, I found a job, but soon I realized that our son's after-school care devoured most of my salary. Whenever a new bill arrived, I worried. I feared that an unexpected emergency would bankrupt us at any minute. We even temporarily ceased giving Sandy an allowance until we could pay off the debts we had incurred during the months we had little income.

Our financial struggles added more strain to my marriage, and some days my husband and I barely spoke. My husband did not turn to me for comfort or caring, and my son acted like an adult. I felt unneeded. I took solace in the greenery I grew on the screened porch of our rental house. My little indoor garden gave me a quiet place where I could escape our financial problems, witness the results of my nurturing, and commune with nature, smack dab in the middle of the city.

Sandy soon learned how to make his own pocket money. With an entrepreneurial spirit, he went door-to-door offering his raking and lawn-mowing skills. He was an industrious seven-year-old. Pleased that Sandy was learning a valuable lesson, I also figured he understood our dire financial situation.

A few days before Mother's Day, he flashed his hazel eyes at me and asked me to take him to a nearby shopping center so he could buy me a gift. I had hoped he would buy something for himself with the few dollars he had scraped together, but his spirit touched me and I agreed to drive him the few miles down the road.

He pointed to a spot outside a variety store. "Wait here, Mom," he instructed.

"Okay," I answered with a smile.

Kids have no corner on curiosity, though, and I soon found myself peeking through the window to see what he was up to. He appeared to be making a beeline toward the lawn-and-garden department, and my heart soared when I saw him duck behind a potted plant and disappear into the darkness of the store. That sweet child of mine knew his mother.

Outside on the sidewalk, I shuffled in the May sunshine, hands deep in my empty pockets, happy to be alive and feeling that things were finally going a little better. After a while, I found myself checking my watch. How long could it take to pick out a plant within his budget? After a few minutes and still no sign of Sandy, I started to worry. What if he had been abducted and taken out a side door? I lingered a few more minutes before panic overpowered me and I dashed to the entrance, only to find him strolling out, a huge smile plastered across his dimpled face. He carried a large cardboard box.

He set it down and looked up at me. "You have to open it right away, Mom. It can't wait till Sunday."

"I understand," I said, knowing the plant could not go long without water and light.

"Okay!" he said, clapping his hands. "Open it now!" He stepped back a little. "Be careful."

"Oh, I'll be very careful, Son."

I leaned down and unfolded the flaps of the box. At first I saw nothing.

My son beamed and waited.

Using my hand to shield my eyes from the sunlight, I stared back into the container. In a dark corner, something moved. I jumped back.

Sandy bent over and pulled out a small brown animal. Its rat tail hung between my son's fingers. "It's a gerbil," he announced with pride.

Slowly, I registered the whole picture—the little rodent and my son, who held it with self-satisfaction. A shopping list flashed through my mind: I had to buy a cage, twenty-five dollars; gerbil food, five dollars;

bedding material, another dollar or two. What else did gerbils need? I had no cash with me at all, only a credit card worn thin from overuse and almost at its limit. I couldn't think of a worse time to bring another mouth into our household, and I could not fathom spending more money to keep the little critter, no matter how adorable its appearance.

The animal's liquid eyes looked up at me with trust. Sandy's eyes sparkled with enthusiasm and excitement. I shifted my thoughts to my son. What would he think and feel when I explained I had to turn around and go back into the store and return the gerbil he'd spent so much time selecting? What would happen to his enthusiasm when I refused his gift? What would he feel about our friendship? Do friends refuse and return gifts given in high spirits?

As I anticipated Sandy's hurt feelings, I could feel them myself. Words escaped me. My throat clamped shut. Tears pooled in my eyes.

My son's ebullience grew. "Oh, Mom! You're crying! I knew you'd love it!" He jumped up and down with joy, clinging to the little creature.

Almost thirty years have passed since that experience, and when I think back on it now, I don't know how, or whether, I ever explained to my husband the presence and expense of that gerbil. I do know we managed to feed it quite well and that it lived with us for years, until it died of old age and was replaced by another. By the time Sandy left for college, we had also raised guppies and puppies, horses and cows, kittens and bunnies, and even a temporarily homeless child. Today, my son has three cats, and I have a dog.

That Mother's Day gift was a microcosm of our life to come. My son and I have stayed good friends. We have always shared a love for living things, be they plants, animals, or people. He even grew up and married a horticulturist. Together, they tend the lush gardens surrounding their house. Oh, and another thing: he became a veterinarian.

Bobbie Christmas

A version of this story was first published as "Happy Mother's Day from My Best Friend" in *On My Mind: A Georgia Writers Anthology, Volume III*, 2001.

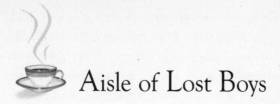 Aisle of Lost Boys

Every time we go to the department store, my twelve-year-old son, Matt, has ten minutes to window-shop the children's book section, the aisle that has picture books, popup books, and other juvenile reading attractions. Although he is allowed to look at these books, we don't buy them. I tell him they are little-kid books and he is a big boy. When I see the look of longing on his face, I feel a twinge of guilt. Is it fair to Matt to deny him ownership of these books? Should he be allowed to stay at the preschool reading level he so enjoys? After all, he has a neurological disability, autism.

Matt can and does read books nearer his grade level, but his old friends really grab his attention. They hold a kaleidoscope of characters and colors that just pop in my son's brain. Simple stories and recognizable characters provide a true comfort zone of reading

244 ~ A Cup of Comfort for Mothers and Sons

for him. But I am determined to stick to my resolve. I think if he were left to his own devices, he would read the same simple books over and over, stuck in an eternal reading loop. He needs to be reading tales that boys his age like. Sports, adventure, and humor for preteens that will stretch his reading experience. Stories that will not only enrich him but will also give him common ground with his peers.

On a recent visit to the store, we were headed toward his favorite book aisle. Ahead of us I spotted a couple, an elderly woman and a middle-aged man. It appeared the man was taking his mother shopping. Their pace was leisurely. Matt's pace was not. He was so excited, he ran ahead of them and into the aisle. Just as the couple passed the same book aisle where Matt stood, the middle-aged man looked at the books and said, "B." My brain tilted. Everything in my perception of them shifted. He didn't say "book," or "Let's look at books," or "I want a book." He said "B." The mother stopped as her slightly balding son walked toward the children's books. Then she slowly turned her cart down the same aisle. I mutely followed.

There the four of us stood. Matt flipped through a Winnie the Pooh book. The middle-aged man looked through an alphabet book. They were years apart in age, yet they stood side by side, entranced by youthful books. His mother and I stood separately, yet together. Two mothers watching two sons, patiently waiting for our boys to finish reading. Fate had placed us there together, watching our forever-young children.

It is an image I do not like to contemplate—my son as Peter Pan forever. But there he stood, right alongside one of the Lost Boys. I glanced at the elderly mother, standing serenely, her white hair perfectly permed and coiffed. Her back was ramrod straight. Her clear eyes looked calm and untroubled. She looked strong and comfortable as her son's mother. I saw years of acceptance etched in the fine smile lines of her face.

And in her face, I saw my future. This would be me in twenty-five years. Older, but still in the kids' book aisle. The awakening glued me to the floor and froze my voice. I wanted to say to her, "I understand why you are here. You must understand why I am here." I wanted to ask her, "How have you managed? What have you done to raise this fine-looking, gentle man? Are you doing okay?" I hoped she didn't think I was staring at her. No words came out of my mouth. It was like a dream when you know you are dreaming, but you want to talk anyway and can't make a sound.

Silently, I thought, *If our children were typical, we wouldn't be here together. We wouldn't be watching our sons in their Neverland.*

Images of what could have been emerged in my imagination. I visualized her picking out a book of nursery rhymes with her grandchild in this same aisle. I imagined myself in the electronics department, watching Matt pick out the latest video game. Would we feel better, worse, or just different if that were allowed us? I want to say it would just be different. I would feel disloyal to Matt if I allowed myself to imagine I would feel better. He is who he is. Matt has no choice in that. I can choose how I feel about him. Part of how I feel is hopeful. Hopeful, because Matt is still young. Hopeful, because I have an undernourished yearning that he may surprise us with as-yet unnoticed abilities. Hopeful he may turn to me someday and say, "Mom, don't worry about me. I'm just fine."

When did that woman lose that hope of a different future for her son? Was he a baby or a teenager? Maybe I didn't really want to connect with her, because I don't want to admit to myself that I am understudying the role she is playing. Would admitting that mean I'd given up hope for Matt's future?

I will never give up hope. Maybe I'm wrong about how she feels; maybe she has hope, too.

It had only been a few minutes since her son first picked up the book he held. He gently returned it to the shelf and turned to his mother. They communicated wordlessly that it was time to move on and walked together out of the aisle. I stood there, silently, while Matt continued to look at books. I wasn't sure I wanted to end his fun. But when his ten minutes were up, I said, "Come on, Matt, let's go," and then I walked away. Abandoning him is the only way to get him out of there. When I walked around the end of the aisle he came running and yelling, "Mom! Mom! Where are you?" I took his hand. Then we walked on together, Wendy and Peter Pan.

Carolyn Carasea

An abbreviated version of this story was first published as "Window Shopping in Time" in *Connection*, January 2003, a newsletter for parents of special-needs students of Green School District, Green, Ohio.

Feet That Leave,
Hearts That Stay

"Mom, I'm not using my middle name at graduation," Jeremy announced matter-of-factly at breakfast one morning during his high school senior year.

"Barret is such a distinguished name," I protested. His dad and I had carefully chosen his names, wanting the perfect combination for our newborn son.

Somehow, with God's grace, I refrained from giving my usual "Mom" lecture. Instead, I smiled.

"Jeremy, your graduation is once in a lifetime. If you don't want to use your middle name, it's okay with me."

"Really? Thanks, Mom. Gotta go." He kissed the top of my head on his way out the door, as was his morning ritual.

Thinking about Jeremy's graduation brought the empty-nest lump to my throat. I had already survived, though painfully, our oldest son's leaving home. I remembered Chris's graduation day. Though it had been a joyful occasion, I was grateful for the extra supply of tissues tucked in my purse.

That summer, I'd winced every time I walked past Chris's nearly empty bedroom and saw the boxes stacked there. The bare walls, once covered with rock-star posters, "Just Do It" inspirations, and pictures of grinning high school athletes, signaled his imminent departure for college. No one had adequately prepared me for this phase of momhood.

I finally mustered the strength to let go, and I'd sent Chris off with wholehearted gladness and prayers for his success. Could I possibly do it again now, with Jeremy? I wasn't so sure. It seemed so recently that we'd first cuddled our sweet baby and pronounced his names for the first time. Now, my youngest son was graduating and dropping one of those names in the ceremony.

Well, I would at least cherish the time Jeremy and I had together. I would show up for every imaginable sports event and sit on those concrete-hard bleachers in the Northwest drizzle. Knowing all too well that next year my calendar would be absent of all those commitments, I would don raingear and huddle with the other moms who also knew the remaining minutes of their mothering days were flying by.

One typical Friday night, Jeremy had a gang of

friends over and invited me to watch a movie with them. "Come on, Mom, you've got to see this one. It's really funny."

I had my doubts, but recognizing another priceless opportunity to spend time with my son, I obliged. We laughed our way through *Throw Momma from the Train*, a wacky comedy about a grown son, Owen, who lives with his incredibly mean mother, Momma.

That's how it all started. Jeremy called me "Momma," and his friends and older brother dubbed him "Owen." We discovered a whole new way of communicating.

"Momma," Jeremy would say in his best Danny DeVito impersonation. "I think you should let me stay out later than midnight. Oh—and by the way, I hate that stuff you're making for dinner tonight." He would add some gagging sounds to make his point.

"Owen," I would respond, trying my best to match Jeremy's acting abilities. "You listen to what I say. I'm your Momma. And you will at least taste the spinach soufflé."

Our playful banter went on for months. "Owen, have you cleaned your room yet? Owen, take out the garbage, please." Of course, my "Momma" character had better manners than my movie counterpart. I even slipped in those sentiments teenage boys avoid like the plague. "Owen, have I told you how much I love you?" His grin told me that he liked my attention.

Weeks slid into months, and the long-anticipated graduation day arrived. We threw a backyard barbecue for Jeremy and his friends, the ones who were often at our house for Friday night movies. Jeremy's proud grandparents helped with the festivities, flipping burgers and slicing the congratulatory cake.

Soon it was time to head for the stadium. I made sure I'd filled my purse with tissues.

"How will we ever find Jeremy?" I lamented.

A sea of 700 green caps and gowns marched across the football field in perfect step to "Pomp and Circumstance." I reached for my purse.

"You're crying already?" my husband said, squeezing my hand.

"I know. I know. I'm supposed to be happy, and I am. I'm just not quite ready to let go," I sniffed. "By the way, Jeremy decided not to use his middle name today."

"Oh?" My husband seemed mildly concerned while adjusting his binoculars.

The school superintendent began reciting the long list of students in Jeremy's graduating class. We strained to hear the familiar name amongst all the others, as we watched for a glimpse of the face we had kissed, wiped peanut butter and jelly off, and dried tears on during his short seventeen years. Then, there was something about the cap perched a bit cockeyed and the familiar gait that told us Jeremy was on the platform, next in line to get his diploma.

The announcer took his name card. His voice boomed over the P.A. system:

"Jeremy—Owen—Kalmbach."

My husband looked at me, and I looked back at him in disbelief. We burst out in laughter until we both needed my tissue stash.

Jeremy looked up at us, his quizzical grin captured forever on film. No matter where he went in life, he would leave his heart with us.

Deb Kalmbach

The Linebacker and the
Sparkly Pink Pumps

One day my three-year-old son, Carlos, saved a toddler at daycare. She was about to dart out into traffic, and he grabbed her by the arm and pulled her to safety. When I found out about it, I was shocked and very proud of him.

"I'll take you to Brook's, and you can get a special hero prize."

He beamed.

As we walked down the toy aisle in the drugstore, Carlos's eyes honed in on a toy, and he tentatively pointed it out to me. "These are cool!" he said quietly.

Glancing over, I saw him take a pair of plastic high heels on a cardboard backing from the hook. They were mules, bright pink and covered with sparkles, with a heart cutout on the toe of each shoe. I hesitated only a moment, then regained my politically correct composure.

"Yeah, they are cool," I said, before nonchalantly adding, "Look at these animal-shaped balloons. . . ."

Now, I should explain that, as an antibias scholar and a bleeding-heart liberal, I strongly oppose gender stereotyping and I have no issue with my son playing with what was considered in my youth to be "girls' toys." I spent my whole childhood wishing for a train set and some Hot Wheels and never getting them. But I also knew how cruel kids could be.

I should also explain that my son is built like a linebacker. He has always been off the charts in height and weight, and he wears the same hat size as my husband. Picturing this solid boy teetering around our house on those Cinderella shoes brought a smile to my face.

"If you want the shoes, honey, you can have them."

He lit up and grasped the package to his chest. As we made our way to the register, I wondered about the consequences of what I had done.

As we drove home, he frantically ripped the pumps out of the package, tore off his hiking boots and socks, and gleefully put them on his feet. Then the proverbial other shoe dropped.

"Mom, can I wear these in to visit Daddy at his work?"

Now, my husband is a contractor, so you can imagine what kind of an audience would be awaiting us.

"No, honey. Those are just to wear at home. I'm

afraid some people might not understand, and I wouldn't want anyone to make fun of you and hurt your feelings. You can wear them around the house all you like."

I don't know whether it was the right thing to say, but he immediately understood and seemed content to limit his fun to the comfort of home.

That afternoon my friend Andrea came over, and immediately her eyes fell on the shoes. I told her the story with a chuckle. She didn't seem as amused.

"Oh, Ann, my husband would be furious with me if I bought those. He would throw them in the garbage and not talk to me for a week!"

I told her I felt I had saved Carlos from an adult shoe fixation, because whenever you deny kids something, without fail, they become obsessed with it. Early that evening my husband walked in, and Carlos rushed up in a flurry of clicking plastic heels to tell Dad about his daring rescue and to show him his new prize. My wonderful husband didn't miss a beat; he looked down, smiled, and congratulated him on his bravery. As he hugged our son hello, my husband looked at me, smiled, and shook his head.

Well, Carlos wore the heels for three straight days, and then threw them in his toy box in the corner of the room and never touched them again. Just before his fifth birthday, Carlos and I were cleaning out his toy box to make room for the new toys he got at

Christmas. He found the shoes in a box under his bed and tossed them onto the pile of toys he wanted to get rid of.

"Those are girls' shoes," he declared, and went back to carefully organizing his Batman toys.

I sighed. I couldn't help but miss that age when he didn't attach a gender to his toys. When he would try out my lipstick and not be ashamed. We try our best to teach our children to be open-minded, but somehow they decide that dolls are for girls and (God help us) guns are for boys. But I can't help but think that the boy in the pink mules is in there somewhere, and that he will, hopefully, grow up to be a sensitive, thoughtful young man who respects differences in people and treats women well. Or at least has really good taste in shoes.

Ann Hagman Cardinal

Boys on the Wall

I n the granite of the Vietnam Veterans' Memorial, I watch the reflection of my husband and two little boys as they whiz past me. The Wall means nothing to my sons, who are four and six. How could they understand a war far away, long ago? How could I understand? I was only a little older than they are now when the war escalated in the late 1960s.

My own memories of the Vietnam War are limited. I wrote to a soldier once when my parents were out and my younger siblings were tucked in bed. He was my babysitter's friend—not her boyfriend, she insisted. I didn't grasp that concept, but I was eager to write a letter in cursive. Pam promised to enclose my letter with hers.

"What should I write?" I asked Pam.

"Just tell him about yourself. He'll appreciate getting mail."

I liked getting mail, too, so in loopy letters, I told the soldier how I loved to read and play solitaire. I asked him to write back. He never did.

I also remember wearing a POW/MIA bracelet in 1972. By that time, about 1,500 soldiers were listed as either prisoners of war or missing in action in Southeast Asia. Like 2 million other Americans, my father, my sisters, my brother, and I put the names of soldiers around our wrists and their plights in our prayers. My dad told us we were supposed to wear them until the soldiers came home. His stainless steel band lasted for two decades. The metal finally wore too thin and snapped. I probably wore my copper bracelet for two months. The metal turned my wrist green. I fiddled with the bracelet, squeezing it tight around my wrist and then pulling it open to take it off. The band broke or I lost it.

I wish I could recall the name of the serviceman I wrote or the name on the bracelet I wore. Then I could look for them along this wall of Williams, Donalds, Kenneths, and Johns—so many Anglo-Saxon names, more reflective of my father's generation than my sons' multicultural contemporaries. Instead, I look for any of the eight women's names among the more than 58,000 and find none.

At the end of the Wall, I flip through pages of the name book under a glass case. The names are listed alphabetically on pages that are clean but slightly crinkled from wear. I look for a family connection, a McKay or a Sener. No matches. Norman, my six-year-old son, interrupts me.

"Mom, come here," he says, tugging on my sleeve. "I have to show you something."

I follow my son to the statue by Frederick E. Hart of three servicemen staring toward the North; the traditional statue was added to the untraditional wall in 1984. *He's probably gawking at the guns,* I think. Two of the soldiers carry rifles almost as big as my son. *Maybe he wants to show me the bullets worn like a safety patrol belt slung over the shoulder of the soldier on the left. Or perhaps he'd like to play count the pockets on the soldiers' pants, which look like the cargo pants in ads for the Gap.*

"Look, Mom," he says. "Look, Mom," he repeats, gazing up at the larger-than-life bronze statue. "They're boys."

Of course. The names on the wall belong to boys, many closer to my son's age than my own. Finally, I feel the power of the Wall. When my son races back to my husband, I let the tears fall. I cry for the mothers, for all the loved ones, and the country still grieving for our boys.

Kathryn McKay

The Beautiful Years

Lately, our home has been overrun with teenage boys. My son, Barrett, who is sixteen, likes to bring his school friends home for lunch. Last week he brought along eight boys. They caught me in my pajamas.

Barrett has an early, eleven o'clock lunch that sneaks up on me very quickly. I was working in my office when everyone came clumping down the stairs. Bags rustled, Tupperware lids popped, and a video began playing amid much laughter, jostling, and joking. I sat frozen in my pink PJs covered with prancing sheep. With a face as rosy as my flannelette, I edged past them and fled upstairs. No one noticed. They are, after all, teenage boys, a species remarkably adept at tuning out the embarrassing behavior of mothers.

Yesterday, Luke and Darcy arrived with Barrett for lunch. They spent almost the whole hour outside.

I watched them through the kitchen window. They dragged a cement slab out of the garage and poured oil over it. Barrett started up his dirt bike, placed the back tire on the oil, and put down the kickstand. Then he proceeded to rev the engine; earlier in the summer he'd removed the muffler, and the sound is deafening. Luke videotaped the action through thick smoke, while Darcy covered his ears and looked on in awe.

I didn't think my son's teenage years would be so utterly delightful. I'm not sure what I expected, but it wasn't the happy-go-lucky world of motorcycles, short-wave radios, computer equipment, electric guitars, and stereos.

I didn't expect to enjoy wandering through Canadian Tire's auto section with a handsome sixteen-year-old towering beside me. I didn't anticipate that, like his great-grandmother, he'd be fond of tea and that some of our most cherished times together would be uptown in the doughnut shop. Least of all, I hardly dared hope the "special night out" tradition I'd started when Barrett was small would mean even more to him as he grew older.

Like other parents, horror stories of rebellion haunted me. But some of the mystery shrouding the process has fallen away. I believe, for the most part, that rebellious behavior doesn't surface unannounced; it gradually moves in over the years until suddenly it's securely lodged in a household. I pray the foundation that has grounded my son since infancy will support him in these years and beyond.

Recently, I saw another world inhabited by teenage boys. A gang war erupted on high school premises; drugs were the issue. Several kids Barrett had gone to school with since kindergarten were involved. Police were called to the scene.

The subject came up a few days later, as Barrett, Darcy, and David were having lunch at our house. Though they hadn't witnessed the event, peers supplied all the details.

"One of the guys had a machete," Darcy announced grandly.

Everyone looked suitably impressed.

"How big was it?" David asked through a mouthful of pepperoni pizza.

"Big," was Darcy's solemn reply.

I hid a smile; it's my guess that sweet little Darcy, the smallest one with the biggest laugh, is unlikely to ever encounter any machete-wielding ruffians.

I found the proximity of evil frightening, yet I also felt peace . . . and a mother's pride. Barrett and his circle of friends aren't involved in these sorts of activities; they've shown no interest in breaking the law or seeking out the company of troublemakers. They've chosen to fill their time with things like snowboarding, renting videos, piling into the hot tub, going to McDonald's, and dirt biking.

These are the beautiful years. This is when every good thing I have ever taught my son is surfacing. He has as many imperfections as anyone, but his heart is good and kind. The manners, lessons, and instructions I repeated ad nauseam when he was tiny have taken root and blossomed. His desire to make right choices fills me with rich, warm joy.

I see a fine young man who works hard and treats others with respect. I see him excelling in school, earnestly planning his future, and hoping his dreams will come true. I see him falling in and out of boyish crushes and spreading wings that are growing stronger each day. Soon, he will discover he is able to soar on his own. I won't be needed to nudge him along and guide his bumpy flight; what a glorious and heartbreaking day that will be.

I'm attempting to make the transition gracefully. A child's adoration has matured; if it weren't so, I'd be concerned. Yet I sometimes yearn for that tender openness and uncomplicated devotion.

A few days ago, Barrett came to an impasse with a personal struggle. Despite my efforts to talk to him, he refused to admit what was wrong. Finally, as I pleaded with him to confide in me, he turned away and started to cry. I put my arms around him. The image will remain imprinted forever upon my memory—a mother overwhelmed with love, tightly holding her boy determined to be a man of integrity, united by an unbreakable bond of unspeakable beauty.

We talked for a long time. The glimpse into the sweetness of his soul was staggering. What a wondrous gift to accompany him into adulthood.

The next day, I bought Barrett a card and filled it with a few paragraphs of how much I treasure and believe in him. I set it on his pillow. A little later, he came down the stairs from his bedroom holding the card. His face was flushed, and his eyes were wet. He was smiling, but his lips trembled. It reminded me of the little boy he used to be.

He thanked me. We hugged, and for the first time he was the last to let go. Funny, I thought, my mind whirling, that a three-dollar card could touch him so deeply. I wish I'd done it sooner.

The teenage journey is seven short years. Here in this extraordinary place, mountains are higher, valleys are lower, and skies are infinite. I don't want to miss any of it. My son and I may not always travel side by side on this great adventure, but we will never be out of each other's reach. For we have miles and miles to go, the two of us. And I have a mother's promises to keep.

Rachel Wallace-Oberle

Pigs in Combat Gear

"If pigs fell out of the sky in combat gear and tried to take over the world, that wouldn't necessarily be impossible."

This is how my son, Sean, begins a conversation. He has just leapt onto the bed where I'd been enjoying the tranquility of a good book and the last rays of the afternoon sun. At eleven, my boy is still in that overgrown puppy stage: all feet and knees and elbows, his gangly legs forever landing him places maturity should direct him to avoid.

"People only think something like that is impossible because they've never seen it happen. But if they saw it, they would." He skips a beat, and then adds, "Mama."

He always tags my name onto the end of the sentence when he thinks I'm either not paying close enough attention or about to laugh.

His instincts are right. Reluctantly, I close my book. "Sure, honey, it wouldn't surprise me a bit to look up and see pigs in army fatigues falling out of an airplane." I widen my eyes in mock awe of his profundity.

"Don't be sarcastic, Mom," he retorts.

I'm proud of his vocabulary and constantly amazed by the creative reach of his young mind. Clearly, he expects some serious thought on this meaty topic.

"Well, scientists have studied pigs' brains, and they just aren't capable of planning something as elaborate as taking over the world. So, I think your scenario is impossible," I say.

He ponders this, and I seize the opportunity to run my hand across his head, enjoying the feel of hair recently shorn with a #5 razor. The back of Sean's neck has always been one of my favorite spots. Since he was a toddler, I have regularly sampled "neck sugar" from this location, grabbing him up and limiting his mobility through a firm headlock before I bite down medium-hard, releasing the sweetness that little boys store there. He fights me, of course, but not too hard. In fact, when the babysitter gave his four-year-old neck a good scrubbing, he met me at the door in tears, afraid she had washed away all of his neck sugar.

My two daughters accuse me of showing favoritism toward their brother, the same complaint I recall voicing to my own mother when I was a child. Here's what I understand now that I didn't then: it's not that I love my son more; it's that I understand him less. Therein lies the fascination.

The girls are like me: their motivations, their fears, their hormone shifts. We have the same body parts. I knew when they were ready to shave their legs and wear their first bras, and how mortified they'd have been if they'd had to bring up the subjects first. I understand the range of their emotions, even why they turn their bathroom counter into a complete disaster area. And when they strive to be unique and separate and completely different from me? I smile at the familiarity of that feeling, too. My daughters read from a script I memorized long ago, a play in which I have been understudy, main attraction, and now lowly light technician. I hold the spotlight on them with steady hands, illuminating their awkward moments, the very ones I would like to change in my past. Raising girls, though a labor of love, is also a chance at redemption.

But giving birth to the male species? What could be more unnatural? I burst into tears when I found out I was pregnant with a boy, and I still can't explain why. It scared me and thrilled me at the same time. Now, I search my son for bits of myself. Sean's hair is dark like mine, his complexion fair and freckled like his daddy's. My eyes are green, but he has widely spaced blue ones, which, he pointed out to me recently, are perfectly centered over the corners of his mouth. He laughs easily, testament to his sunny nature, and I claim that trait along with his sense of humor, keen powers of observation, and inquisitive nature. My husband disagrees, saying all the good characteristics came from his side of the family, and my mother-in-law, traitor to the cause, dredges up photos and anecdotes to prove his point.

Though he wants to be a professional baseball player, I hold fast to the dream that my son will become a writer someday, since there is no genetic possibility of linking this talent to his father's family. More than I ever did with my daughters, I encourage his inclinations in this area, praising him for keeping a journal and feeding him tidbits for stories. His recent observations give me hope.

Watching a pot of soup simmering on the stove, he remarked, "There's a mime in there."

I thought I had misunderstood him, but then he lifted up his arms, palms flat and facing the ceiling, and copied the gentle boil of the soup, which did, indeed, look like a mime pushing upward on the surface of the hot liquid. The moment passed as he rushed out the door, tackling the dog and rolling on the freshly mown grass, which all too soon he would track back into the house.

Underneath Sean's gentle spirit lurks the potential for aggression, the strength nature has given him to be the protector of his own kids someday. I instinctively hold it at bay, postponing the time when I must inevitably accept the certainty of his rampant Y chromosome. I know he will be a man soon enough, but it's his innocence I embrace today. We wrestle on the bed, a format acceptable for displaying affection with a son. I pin his arms above his head and nibble on his belly. He counters by making a game of poking his finger at my mouth, daring me to catch it in my teeth. I succeed in biting first his finger, then his wrist, leaving my teeth prints in his young flesh.

"You bit my vein!" he squeals, delighting in the physical contact, the pleasure bordering on pain.

We improvise a skit in which we explain to the paramedic why he must be rushed to surgery to repair a vein pierced by a vicious animal, his mother.

"But if they came from Pluto, they could be like a whole different species. What if they had advanced technology? Then they might take over the world." Deep breath. "Mama."

We're back to the pigs—Plutonian, this time; the probability of the impossible, the likelihood of the unlikely.

I'm suddenly grateful for my son's freedom to dwell on the absurd. Life will throw him the inevitable curveball someday, and he'll rise to the occasion, strong, capable, ready for battle. My job as his mother is to protect his vulnerability, to nurture the little boy in him, no matter how old he gets. What could be more impossible than a woman giving birth to a man-child, so foreign, so different from herself? What could be less likely than a mother's drive to foster her son's weakest parts, and in so doing, prepare him for the vocation of manhood?

I feel his warm breath on my neck as he awaits my answer.

"You know, Son, stranger things have happened," I confess. "When you put it that way, I think it just might be possible. Maybe pigs *can* fall from the sky in combat gear."

Ellen H. Ward

Sons and Streams

I have three sons.

And in my dreams we are on the Queets River, fishing, casting out long, crystal lines into the water. The lines drift down clear rivulets and bump against smooth gray rocks slick with moss. The forest of cedar and spruce at the river's edge is deep and wild. The boys are young, and they gather at their father's wading boots like goslings under gander wings.

I sit on the mossy bank and sketch, shaded by massive spruce as old as Time. At night, I read *The Lord of the Rings* to the boys by flashlight and firelight. The sparks rise up like fireflies and disappear into the starsplashed sky above the sleeping firs and pines.

We are together, and we are whole.

Someone once wrote that the mother of three sons has a special place in heaven. I have never felt such a burden, but rather, have relished each individual life as it came to me at birth. Their personalities were as telling as when they first suckled: one had to figure it out, one was ready to go, and one held my finger in his tiny hand.

My nana had three sons. Well, actually four. Her firstborn died a baby boy after eating green corn on a summer day long ago. I see her now in her Gibson Girl skirt and shirtwaist, casting out her line into a river in Colorado. She is wearing a hat more fashionable than a sun stopper. The water's edge is flat and bare with few trees. The sun beats down from the cloudless sky. She is looking upriver at my grandfather, who is fishing in tweeds with his hand on his hip. At her feet, my knickers-wearing uncles tie their bait to their Spanish gut lines on bamboo poles. They are young and full of adventure, ready to do more than throw a line into the low-riding river, but Nana is patient. She fishes and waits.

What is a mother to a bevy of boys? A gaggle of guys?

I dreamed of a girl. There was a tradition in my side of the family of women handing down their stories and treasures. At my mother's house, there is a box with a ship made of gesso on top; handmade lace spun from homegrown flax; Nana's china dolls with exquisite silk dresses and tiny brass buttons, thimbles from 150 years ago, and letters and poems. We named our girl Robin Lynn each time I was pregnant, but when the doctor told me that my third child would most likely be a boy, I put aside that dream and looked to the ease of hand-me-downs and the familiarity of raising boys.

From the time they could walk or ride in a backpack, we fished, camped, and hiked in the deep forests of the North Cascades, finding our way on fish trails to alpine lakes tucked under craggy peaks. Or we went to the Queets and the Hoh on the Olympic Peninsula, where the salmon flung their way upstream to their end. Their father was always there, his fishing and camping wisdom the backbone of their education. I showed them history in the occasional ruined cabin, the springboard notch in the ancient cedar stump; sang songs and told stories.

The year we crossed the Queets, my youngest was tall enough to ford it, the water coming up just below his small backpack. We hiked north through dense Pacific Northwest rainforest. I took pictures with a cheap camera, and the images, though bright with the reds and blues of the boys' rain jackets and deep greens of woods, blurred. But memory is stronger and brings each image back as sharp as when they were first shot. The boys perched on a huge beached driftwood tree. My oldest, with his Swedish blond hair cut into a fifties crew cut, proudly holding up a salmon as tall as he is. My middle son with his first salmon cradled in his arms like a treasured puppy—just as the ranger arrived to check on fishing licenses. He didn't have one, but it was his first, and his joy turned the official's other cheek. Later, my youngest caught one, too. With his dad's catches, we carried out nearly fifty-eight pounds of fish.

Three sons, as solid as a triangle. Three has always been my favorite number.

And then my husband suddenly died.

At first, we huddled together like harried sheep, numbly going through the paces of grief and braving the holiday season so lacking in cheer. But in time each son had to make his way back to his own life, two in other towns. There, they grieved in different ways. One thought of quitting college. Another rolled up in his blankets and avoided work. The third began to implode. The triangle could not hold.

Losing your father can be devastating to a young man in his early twenties. It is a time when he is finally beginning to figure things out and step into true manhood. A time when he is ready to listen to his father's advice.

What is a mother to sons without a father? How do you lead when your own heart mourns?

I went forward, encouraging them each to move forward and go for their dreams, and I set out toward some dreams of my own. By Thanksgiving the year after my husband died, we were gathered at the table with friends and working hard at creating happiness.

We laughed, played Scrabble, and went en masse to see *Harry Potter*, though we were restless, waiting for *The Lord of the Rings: The Two Towers*.

New Year's came. Hopes were raised. One son had finished school and was engaged to be married. Another had chosen to leave work for grad school. The third slept, and we didn't recognize the storm that was to come. Two months later, his raging grief of months literally exploded in a shattering of glass when he threw himself out a window. The triangle was broken.

Dealing with a serious crisis with a child is difficult enough as a parent. The grief of facing it alone is even worse, especially when the parent is a mother and the child a son. Society dictates that the relationship should grow less influential as the boy matures into manhood. He should turn to his father. Moms are for Mother's Day.

After my husband died, I grieved for what I had lost. But I also grieved out of fear that somehow I would lose my sons as well, as they went off on their own paths in their lives.

But the days and nights of just being there for my troubled young-adult son—at the emergency room, by the hospital bed, on the phone—has brought me better understanding and wisdom of what it is to be a mother to sons. It takes courage I did not know I had. It means listening, staying silent when nothing more needs to be said, to provide a foundation of support without enabling when all else fails for that person; to let go.

My nana knew grief. The grief for a precious baby who died so young from an illness cured easily today with salt and sugar water; for a young son with appendicitis sent off on a Pocatello train, thinking she'd never see him again; and for sons gone off to fight in trenches in World War I. And when she, nearly ninety-five years old and most in need, lived beyond them.

I see her on the river, the boys crouched at her feet. The future is ahead of her, and she is looking with pole in hand.

Sons and streams.

That is something I know, and she gives me strength. Is not our whole life a stream on which we drift?

I have three sons.

And in my dreams we are together again, battered but together on the Queets. We may not fish. The poles and tackle boxes are in my garage, and the water rushing down at high water keeps us from going across. But we will put some of their father's ashes there and watch the eagles in the trees as they welcome him. I do not know the future, but I hope for forgiveness and healing. I hope for wholeness. And my three sons gathering around.

Janet L. Oakley

 Reverse Psychology

My firstborn, Scott, would have been a challenge for any mother. For a brand-new mom with little child-rearing know-how, he was, as they say, "a handful." With an intelligence and a sense of humor that exceeded his years, combined with an energy and a curiosity that topped the charts, Scott managed to find mischief where no mischief had gone before. So it was that, shortly after this whimsical little man came into my life, I found myself buried in how-to books on disciplining children, raising responsible kids, tough love, and other parenting advice. As time went on and Scott's antics continued and, if anything, became more creative, my realm of study expanded to include child psychology classes as well as listening to parenting tapes and radio programs.

Now, don't get me wrong; Scott was not a "bad" kid. He wasn't malicious, he didn't deliberately look for trouble, and he wasn't a nonstop challenge, 24/7. In those fleeting moments when he wasn't pulling pranks or being rambunctious, he could be a downright sweetheart. But he was very active and more than a little ornery, and he had an uncanny ability to outsmart other people. Not many children regard April Fool's Day with as much enthusiasm as they do Christmas.

Staying a step ahead of my wily male child was not only challenging, it was, at times, next to impossible—especially as our family grew to two, then three, then four children. That's when the books in my library started changing from how-tos to "how comes."

Just when I thought I'd reached the end of my parental resources, and rope, with Scott, I happened upon a radio talk show hosted by a well-known child psychologist, Dr. James Dobson. Impressed with his apparent expertise, I immediately went out and purchased a set of his audiotapes. Whenever the rare opportunity arose for me to listen and learn, I did so eagerly.

One weekend, my mom and dad invited Scott to their house for a sleepover. With my little mastermind out of my hair—er, the house—for a day or so, I finally had the opportunity to soak up a few of Dr. Dobson's tapes. One particular tape, which focused on handling a challenging child and gaining his or her respect, really piqued my interest.

In that session, Dr. Dobson used an experience from his own childhood to illustrate how his mother had applied "reverse psychology" to show him how she felt when she had to discipline him. Mesmerized, I listened as he explained the concept and described his youthful turnabout.

He had done something naughty and was standing before his mother, anticipating his punishment. She held in her hand a paddle. But before administering the blows, she had something to say to her young son—the proverbial "heart-to-heart talk" most kids dread but often dismiss. She told him that, to have a son who was constantly compelled to get into mischief, she must not be a good mother . . . and so, being a bad mother, *she* should be the one to receive punishment. Now, she instructed solemnly, it was up to him to spank her.

He gasped in horror! Spank his mother? The person who had rocked him and nursed him as a babe, who read stories to him, fed him, mended his hurts, dried his tears, attended his sporting events, and rubbed his back until he fell asleep at night? How could he possibly spank his mom, who loved him so much, to atone for his mistake?

Tears rolled down his cheeks as she handed him the paddle. He didn't want to spank her. He didn't want to hurt her, ever. She was his mom, and he loved her. In that moment, he realized how his mother must have felt every time she had to spank him. And he vowed to try harder not to give her reason to punish him again.

Needless to say, he didn't spank her. And, of course, he didn't never again do anything wrong. No child is that perfect. But he learned a big lesson that day, which inspired him to improve his behavior and to think before he acted out, and which gave him a new respect for his mom.

Eureka! This was the answer I'd been looking for to teach my little Scott a new attitude toward his mommy. I almost couldn't wait until he misbehaved again, so I could administer this very valuable lesson.

Upon Scott's return home from Grandma and Grandpa's house, it didn't take long before he was tormenting his three sisters again and the opportunity arose for me to put my plan into action. If there was an Oscar for "actress playing a sorrowful mother," I would have received it. As a tear rolled down my cheek, I took Scott by one hand, and gripping the paddle in the other, led him into the "time out" room. I knelt before him and said my well-practiced lines.

"Scott," I began. "I must not be a very good mommy to you. No matter what I try to do to help you stop picking on your sisters, you just don't seem to listen. It hurts me inside to think you don't want to behave. It makes me feel like I'm a bad mommy."

For the first time in his little life, he stood before

me quietly, truly listening to my words. It was hard for me not to chuckle under my breath, but I was going for broke here. I continued:

"My son, I hope you can forgive me for being a bad mommy. God wants me to be a good mommy to you, not a bad mommy. So, I feel I am the one who deserves a spanking today."

With that, another tear rolled down my cheek, and I stood up. I handed him the paddle. His eyes widened in what appeared to be horror. Slowly, I turned my back to him and then bent over.

My heart was pounding so hard I thought it would jump out of my chest. Moments passed in what seemed like hours, and I started reveling in the knowledge that Scott had learned a valuable lesson, and planned on boasting of my success to his daddy. With my back turned to my seven-year-old son, I envisioned his sad face, how he was going to beg my forgiveness and promise to change, how he—

Whack!

What was that stinging reality I'd just felt?

Whack!

No! As I turned to look at my son, it dawned on me that the look I'd construed as horror wasn't horror at all—it was euphoria! He wasn't begging for my forgiveness. He wasn't saddened by this course of events. He was basking in sheer delight!

Whack!

I began to run! He began to chase me!

Having never been allowed to hold the paddle in his hands before, he was now wielding it like a weapon and loving every second of it. Glancing behind me, all I could see was the blur of his Cheshire-cat smile and his spindly legs carrying him wildly closer.

Any hope I'd had of teaching my son a lesson flew straight out the door—with me right behind it and my son in hot pursuit. I don't remember how many neighborhood blocks he chased me before I finally turned, tackled him, and wrestled the paddle from his grip. What I do know is that it wasn't my son who learned a lesson that day.

Though I didn't win any acting or parenting awards for that performance, I did put reverse psychology back where it belonged—in the psychologist's office. And I did learn, in due time, that the real guide to raising a responsible, loving son comes from understanding, and accepting, and loving, and nurturing who he is, as an individual.

Today, my son and I are very close, and I am extremely proud of the man he has become. He and my daughters are my pride and joy—never mind the sometimes rocky road we traveled to get here. We often reminisce about their childhood escapades. Scott naturally lays claim to more than his fair share, and he inevitably retells the mommy-spanking debacle, always amidst gales of laughter. But perhaps I will get the last laugh, after all.

You see, Scott is now the proud father of a wily, strong-willed, beautiful two-year-old little girl. Perhaps for his birthday, I will give him my collection of Dr. Dobson tapes.

Cheryl Glowacki

 # She Did Everything

When I was a graduate student at the University of Iowa, I had more than my share of student athletes in my classes. Like most people, I'd heard the cliché of the dumb jock. I was pleasantly surprised to discover that the athletes at Iowa were almost uniformly pleasant and respectful, and most were above-average students. There were, however, a few who weren't that interested in academics. They were at college primarily to play sports and school took a distant second place in their loyalties.

Jeremy fell into that category. As long as his grades were high enough to keep him on the football team, that's all he cared about. I wanted to see him catch fire academically as well, and I cast about for assignments that might appeal to him and my other athletes.

I was teaching rhetoric and decided to ask them to do a ceremonial speech.

"I want you to give a speech thanking someone who is really important to you, or celebrating a great achievement, or honoring someone who helped you become the person you are today. Go wild here. Let your imaginations flow."

Until then, the only questions Jeremy had asked me were those regarding due dates. That day, he was waiting after the end of class to ask questions.

"I, um, I don't know what to give a speech about. I do better when you tell me what to write," he said.

"Well, I can't do that this time," I said. "This speech has to be yours. It's about the thing that is most important to you. What is that?"

"Football."

"So, give a speech about football."

"What would I say?"

"Did you have a coach who inspired you?"

"No."

"Did your dad help you play when you were young?"

"Don't have a dad."

"Well, did anybody help you become the person you are today?"

"No, sir," he said. "Everything I have, I earned. I lifted the weights. I took the hits."

If ever someone believed in the self-made man, it was Jeremy. And he almost convinced me. I tried one more time. "What about your mom?"

Jeremy's face lit up like that of a five-year-old who's been asked to name his favorite toy. "Help? She did everything. She didn't know anything about football, but she went out in the backyard after work and threw the ball with me until it got dark. She raised us alone, working two jobs, but she never missed a practice. She helped me stand up straight; she made me proud. And she always encouraged me."

He went on for quite some time. The room was about half full with the next class by the time he finished with, "There's nothing my mom didn't help me with. I wouldn't be anything if it weren't for her. How could I have been so stupid?"

Needless to say, Jeremy's ceremonial speech was one of gratitude to his mother. His delivery was passionate, and he drilled his speech like it was a new play on the football field, which meant it was perfect. He did this without losing his open heart, which meant that my class got to bask in the sight of a six-foot-six brute crooning his love for his mother, once stopping because he was close to tears. His speech earned him an A and several spontaneous handshakes from classmates who were so moved they said they were going to call their parents after class.

Jeremy gave his mother the gift of the respect she deserved. He gave his classmates a gift as well, by sharing his emotions with them and shattering stereotypes of what it means to be male. And finally, though he did not know it, Jeremy gave me a gift as well.

I work hard to produce assignments that fulfill course objectives, assignments that fit together logically to methodically build the core skills a course is intended to develop. I like those qualities, and I still try to design assignments that do those things. But after Jeremy, I also remember to help my students unlock the door to the wonderful passion already inside them. In Jeremy's case, that meant unlocking the door that kept him from realizing how much his mother had already given him. She was the most important mentor in his life, far more important than any coach or teacher could ever be.

In sharing that insight with me, Jeremy unlocked a door for me as a teacher. As important, he also reminded me of a lesson many of us—being busy boys obsessed with winning our games, whether they be sports, like football, or our careers—need to remember and too often forget. Jeremy reminded me that, without our mothers, we wouldn't be here, and that, in many cases, she didn't just help. She did everything.

Greg Beatty

 I Linger

A Bugs Bunny lamp is the only light as I move slowly toward my son's bed, my eyes adjusting to the darkness. Books, lying open where they were haphazardly thrown, litter the floor, and I lightly step over them. I tuck the satiny edge of his blanket around his shoulders and sit on the edge of his bed, as he moves his legs to give me room. The mattress sinks as I settle in. It is old, having followed me into my marriage and out again, and feels soft. I think of the backache I would wake up with were I tempted to sleep here all night.

I place my hand on my son and instinctively begin to rub his back through a layer of sheets, blankets, and one of my T-shirts, his recently adopted pajamas.

"I like the way it smells," he said when I tried to trade it for his Ninja Turtle pajamas. "And it helps me go back to sleep after I have a bad dream."

He has nightmares often, violent dreams that are a mix of cartoon-character battles and frightening news clips, and I am often awakened by the sound of his footsteps hopping out of bed and scurrying into my room. I lift my blankets to receive him even before he reaches me, and as he climbs in, I wrap my arms around his warm body. Nuzzling his hair, I kiss his head, and in our comfort, we fall back to sleep.

"Can you feel my hand through all this padding?" I ask, as I continue rubbing his back.

"Um-hmm," he answers.

This is our bedtime ritual, born of my divorce from his father last year, at a time of need for both of us. With the rest of his world full of upheaval, my son needed a routine to look forward to and rely on. And I needed a quiet, slow time with my child while the rest of my life was being bombarded with change. There was my new job, his new school, and now our second move in a year. Bedtime became our constant.

Tonight he has already played, eaten his dinner, taken his bath, and brushed his teeth. We've talked about what happened at school today and who is picking him up where tomorrow. Now, it's our time, when we leave the rest of the world outside his bedroom door.

We choose the song we will sing, knowing it will be the same one chosen every night since I began singing it almost ten months ago at Christmas. I softly begin, and he joins me.

"Silent night, holy night," we sing. The sound of our voices off-key together offends my sense of hearing but warms my heart.

As we sing, I look at the Batman poster on the wall across from his bed. The lower left-hand corner is torn away, and the thumbtack holding it in place has been used for some boyish experiment. His dream catcher hangs above his head, with its tiny feathers ruffling in the breeze from the open window. A light gust blows a scrap of paper toward the closet, and I notice his G.I. Joe stuck in the netting of a plastic basketball hoop. He hangs in an awkward pose, grasping at the orange frame with his tiny rubber fingers.

Dirty pants, socks, and shirts surround his hamper in heaps, where he tossed them in failed basketball shots. We have had many discussions about his clothes landing in the hamper, not around it, but tonight I simply smile at his consistency.

We've reached the "round yon virgin" verse now, and I wonder when he will question me about the word "virgin" and what it means. I am reminded of our drive home from school yesterday when he asked, "Mom, what's a hard-on?" I searched for a well-thought-out and informative, yet not too descriptive, explanation.

"Well, when a man, or a boy, gets ah . . . ," I stammered as we pulled into our driveway, "excited . . . and, ah . . ."

"Hey, Mom! Jason's here," my son interrupted. "Can I stay outside and play?"

"You bet," I replied with a sense of relief. Now I would have an opportunity to give the answer some thought before it was asked again.

As our song draws to an end, he yawns, and his voice softens.

"Once more, please?" he asks, his dark eyelashes whispering as his eyelids flutter.

I brush wisps of hair away from his cheeks and notice how tan his face has become over the summer. It was a summer of new schedules, as he spent most of his time at his dad's house. I would pick him up for our treasured weekends together, and he would chatter about the polliwogs in the river or a new television cartoon. Then his voice would become a whisper, and I would lean toward him as he told me how he'd cried at night when he missed me. I didn't tell him about the tears I cried on my drive home every Sunday or how I always made sure to pack one of my T-shirts in his suitcase for him.

His brow furrows, and I caress it gently, trying to pull the worries into my own hands. Do I ride the bus home, or is Dad picking me up? What if Dad doesn't see me and he leaves? Whose house am I staying at tomorrow night? Will Dad take me to my soccer game? Questions that overwhelm the normal childhood inquiries of hot lunch versus cold lunch and when is recess.

I gaze into my son's face as his eyelids finally close, and I finish the song alone. Nestling his head against his Power Rangers pillowcase, he slips into sleep's open arms, and the memory of earlier disagreements over homework and chores fade. I lean over and gently touch my lips to his forehead. He responds with a half-hearted hug, his arms comforting around my neck, and I linger, inhaling the smell of strawberry shampoo and toothpaste . . . the smell of him.

Tricia L. McDonald

Bedraggled, Bedeviled, and Beguiled

After another long day at the office, I made a quick stop at the grocery store, picked up my youngest child at daycare, and finally arrived home, hoping to find my daughter and two older sons in the house doing their homework. I stood Logan on his wobbly toddler legs, scooped up the groceries, and tried to steer my two-year-old toward the front door, nearly dropping one of the three grocery sacks.

"Logan, honey, please go to the house. . . . That's right. . . . Go see if your brothers are home."

I almost made it to the door with groceries and child intact, when both dogs came roaring around the corner, knocked over the baby, and jumped at me in a frantic attempt to lick my face. Giving up, I dropped the sacks, pulled Logan out of the way of the rambunctious dogs, and bent down to dry my little one's sudden tears.

Then I heard the bone-chilling call from the backyard.

"Mom! Help! I'm hurt!"

Abandoning the groceries on the sidewalk, I tore through the house with the dogs at my heels, set the baby on the floor as I passed through the living room, and sprinted out the back door.

"Marsh! What happened—?" I took one look at his nose lying sideways on his face and nearly fainted. "Oh, my God. Here, Son, come into the house."

The story came out in pieces.

"I found a heavy boat anchor," he gasped. "It had this really long rope tied to it."

I sat him on the couch, ran to get a bag of ice, wrapped the ice pack in a towel, and dashed back to the living room.

". . . I wanted the anchor to hang from that tall branch in the tree behind our house. So I started swinging it around and around."

I handed him the ice pack.

". . . When the anchor picked up enough speed, I let go of it."

Wincing, he placed the bag on his nose, and sounding a little muffled, he continued his tale.

". . . The anchor flew really high in the air, up and over the branch." He sniffled, wincing again. "But then it came flying back at me and hit me right in the face!"

"Oh, honey." I shuddered, and then forced myself to get my bearings. "Okay, keep holding the ice on your nose while I call the doctor and see what we should do."

On the way to the kitchen to get the phone, I caught a glimpse of Logan standing in the bathroom just off the kitchen, joyfully dunking his shoe in the toilet.

"Logan! No!" I reached him a split second before he flushed. "Go into the living room with Marsh. I'll be there in a minute."

After retrieving the tennis shoe out of the toilet, I dropped the soggy mess into the washing machine and headed, once more, for the telephone.

"Mom! This is cold! Can't I take it off now?"

Starting to feel a little ragged, I kicked off my high heels and called out, "No, leave it on a little longer, Marsh. I need to call the doctor. Hang in there."

Just as I reached for the receiver, the phone rang. Rolling my eyes toward heaven, I silently asked God to help me and picked up the phone.

"Hello?"

"Lori? This is Helen in the apartment manager's office."

"Hello, Helen. How are you?"

"I'm fine. But, well, your son Ryan is up here on the main road mooning people as they drive by."

I hung my head, closed my eyes, and wished for

Calgon to take me away. Taking a deep breath, I said, "Okay, Helen, I'll be right there."

But Helen decided to take that inopportune moment to let me know what a lousy job as mother she thought I was doing. "Lori, I have to tell you. You need to keep those boys under control."

"Yes, Helen." I bit my tongue fiercely, struggling to contain my emotions. It didn't work. "Maybe," I added dryly, "I'll just Super Glue his pants to his butt from now on."

I made a face at the phone as she made a strangled noise, then I said as sweetly as possible, "I'll take care of it."

This was not an unusual day at my household. With three sons, a teenage daughter, two dogs, an ex-husband who lives in a different town, and a full-time job, it was pretty much my life as usual—every single day.

Marsh was always curious and adventurous, a born leader. Ryan, two years younger but big for his age and twice as tough, ran with his older brother and their band of merry adventurers.

They were ornery, I fully admit. Most people watching from afar might even have thought them rather rotten. But my mother's eye saw the good in them. They never really hurt a soul, and for every prank they pulled, they did a few nice things, too. They carried in groceries for elderly neighbors, and when it snowed they cleared their sidewalks. They protected the younger, weaker kids from neighborhood bullies, and they shared whatever they had with their friends. And they loved their mom so much they would rush home to take detention slips out of the mailbox before I came home from a hard day's work to find them. Of course, I was unaware of this last act of consideration until many years later, when my rowdy boys, now men, finally copped to it.

It was also some time before other stories began to surface about exactly how audacious they had truly been.

Apparently, there were many summer nights when they escaped from their second-story room by jumping out of the window. They would run to meet their friends, who had gotten out of their homes in the same manner.

It seems they often climbed to the top of the neighborhood grocery store and dropped water balloons on patrons. When the police were summoned, they would slide down the water pipes and fire escapes. They even dug tunnels in the field behind our house so they could hide when the police came too close. My stomach nearly overturned when they told me about the king snake they found while digging these escape tunnels—and that, of course, they had brought it home and secretly kept it under their bunk bed as a pet.

Recently, they told the tale of the night they were nearly caught by the police. It seems they had been shooting their Fourth of July stash of fireworks at passing police cars, when the police made an all-out attempt to finally catch the devilish rascals. But alas, the chase was grown men against wiry boys, and they managed to elude the police by jumping fences and running across backyards. Laughingly, they related their favorite part of the story: When they jumped over a privacy fence into one particular backyard, they apparently interrupted an older couple having a friendly interlude in the hot tub. When the silver-haired, bearded, portly gentleman jumped from the hot tub completely in the buff, the boys catapulted over his fence into the neighboring yard and ran through the next neighborhood before collapsing into a pile of giggling fools on yet someone else's lawn. It was then one of them gasped out, "I think we just saw Santa Claus . . . naked!" Turning their giggles into guffaws.

And where, you might ask, was I? I was sleeping peacefully, thankful that my little darlings were asleep in their beds. At the beginning of my adult life, if God had sent me a memo saying I would give birth to sons and if I had known then what I know now, would I have run screaming in the other direction? Possibly.

But if I had, I would have missed what I think of as my great reward. That arrived on a Mother's Day when Ryan and Marsh were young men on the brink of adulthood.

Ryan came into the room first. He had grown into what I always knew he could be—a loving, responsible young man. He handed me a beautiful bouquet of roses. The little card snuggled among the baby's breath and red blossoms said simply, "I love you, Mom." As I was telling him I loved him, too, his brother walked into the room.

Marsh, then a college junior, smiled and wrinkled his now slightly crooked nose before presenting me with a book especially for mothers. But it was the card accompanying his gift that, years later, still brings tears to my eyes. In Marsh's scrawling script it reads:

Mom,
    Even though you never knew what we were up to, I always knew that if I had gotten caught, you would still love me. Thanks for putting up with me.
    I love you.
    Marsh

Had I known then what I know now, would I do it all again? Without a doubt.

Lori Bottoms

# Using Our Words

My son and I have great conversations.

Early on, we engaged in creative exchanges filled with made-up words and facsimiles of real ones he had trouble getting his little tongue around. Toward the end of his second year, as we waited for the holidays, he answered the question, "What would you like for Christmas?" with a multisyllable, one-word reply.

"Ingabritz!"

"An 'ingabritz'?"

"I want an ingabritz."

That was a stumper.

A few days before the big day, while we were running errands, a siren screamed behind us, and I quickly pulled the car over to the side of the road. A blinking, blaring flash of red and white whizzed by.

"Ingabritz! Ingabritz!" my son called out.

Message decoded. The biggest, shiniest ambulance I could find was under the tree that Christmas.

Our days were filled with words. Silly songs, nonsense rhymes, and story times were punctuated with tickles and giggles. I respectfully addressed all his stuffed animal buddies by their given names. Taking a walk through the neighborhood together, we imagined what the dogs would say if they could talk. What did the geraniums in Grandma's flower boxes whisper to each other when no one was listening? Even his blocks and puzzles led to word play, with, "What are you building over there?" eliciting the most fantastic stories.

When he went off to preschool, I was treated to gaudy creations adorned with cotton-ball clouds and Popsicle-stick people stuck all over with string and sparkles. Then came the week he brought home nothing but construction-paper canvases of scenes drawn in black or mud brown. How I fretted over the dismal drawings, my overactive imagination ascribing psychological undertones not easily associated with this generally happy boy. I paged through a sizable stack of parenting books, searching for fresh ways to stimulate his creativity. Day after day, he dropped a backpack filled with monochromes on the kitchen chair. On Friday, when I finally asked what had happened to all the cheery rainbow colors he loved, the answer was simple: He was usually the last one to the crayon box, so only the black and brown crayons were left.

Then we talked about his pictures. Scooting close, he enthusiastically pointed out the red house, blue sky, and beaming yellow sun. We pored over another one, and he described tall green trees and a pond, a little boy standing near the edge.

"What color is the water?" I asked.

"Dark blue, Mom," he replied, reaching for a miniature car across the table, already on to something much more interesting.

Dark blue. That accounted for the sinister black circle in the center of the sheet. His slender fingers may have been guiding a dreary-colored crayon, but his extraordinary child's mind had been concocting vibrant works of art. He saw the colors. I was the one who was mistakenly taking things at face value rather than recognizing the creative possibilities. He used his words to help me understand.

We continued to talk all through the school years. There were milestone discussions and ordinary conversations. I don't remember awkward moments or subjects that were off-limits. Unlike with many mothers and sons, our lines of communication remained open.

He traded Ohio for Oregon when he went off to college. Phone calls were short and sweet and occasionally spilling over with exciting plans. On a visit to his new home away from home, we explored lush forests and followed the sounds—first distant, then thunderous—to discover hidden waterfalls.

When my father suffered a massive heart attack, a life-support system sustained his breathing while the family made difficult decisions no one ever wants to face. Late one night, my son and I visited. I talked to Pop awhile, then left the room so Grandfather and Grandson could share some quiet time like they used to, hoeing in the vegetable garden or pulling fish out of the small lake lined with retirement homes.

Though the conversation was one-sided, there was no lack of animation. The young man read the sports page, commenting on the trades, the scores, and the behind-the-scenes of what was, for some, an ordinary day in the January world of football, basketball, and hockey. For a mother, proud of her son, it was an extraordinary night. We talked a little, mostly with our eyes, showing each other how much we cared for this special man and for each other. There were no words, really. Those could wait for another day.

When the breast cancer diagnosis came, we discussed the unwelcome surprise in clinical and emotional terms. One day an e-mail arrived with "This One's for You, Mom" in the subject line and a photo attached. His image spoke volumes: a smiling face, hat on backward, number on his chest, racing for the cure.

He's lived and worked in Europe, survived the dot.com crash, and carved out a spot for himself in the fast-paced corporate world. He's going to be thirty soon. Imagine that.

We live in different cities and call back and forth regularly. The subjects of our conversations are appropriately adult now. We mull over stock options and retirement plans, and bring each other up-to-date on family news. One evening I propose something new.

"How about meeting someplace warm and wonderful for Christmas this year? A beach? Palm trees? Snorkeling? Think about where you'd like to go."

"You know, Mom, I don't need to think about it," says the traditionalist. "I like coming home for Christmas."

He has more plans for the future. Sometimes they make me think of the little guy whose "red" house boldly filled the page.

Of course, we don't talk every day like we did when he was small. But we still speak the same language—words of hope, fun, trust, comfort, love. They color our lives with exciting possibilities. Many years ago, a little boy taught me that.

Marge D. Hansen

Tell Your Story in the Next *Cup of Comfort*!

We hope you have enjoyed *A Cup of Comfort for Mothers & Sons* and that you will share it with all the special people in your life.

You won't want to miss our next heartwarming volumes, *A Cup of Comfort for Christians* and *A Cup of Comfort for Grandparents*. Look for these new books in your favorite bookstores soon!

We're brewing up lots of other *Cup of Comfort* books, each filled to the brim with true stories that will touch your heart and soothe your soul. The inspiring tales included in these collections are written by everyday men and women, and we would love to include one of your stories in an upcoming edition of *A Cup of Comfort*.

Do you have a powerful story about an experience that dramatically changed or enhanced your life? A compelling story that can stir our emotions, make us think, and bring us hope? An inspiring story that reveals lessons of humility within a vividly told tale? Tell us your story!

Each *Cup of Comfort* contributor will receive a monetary fee, author credit, and a complimentary copy of the book. Just e-mail your submission of 1,000 to 2,000 words (one story per e-mail; no attachments, please) to:

cupofcomfort@adamsmedia.com

Or, if e-mail is unavailable to you, send it to:

A Cup of Comfort
Adams Media
57 Littlefield Street
Avon, MA 02322

You can submit as many stories as you'd like, for whichever volumes you'd like. Make sure to include your name, address, and other contact information and indicate for which volume you'd like your story to be considered. We also welcome your suggestions or stories for new *Cup of Comfort* themes.

For more information, please visit our Web site: *www.cupofcomfort.com.*

We look forward to sharing many more soothing *Cups of Comfort* with you!

Contributors

Greg Beatty ("She Did Everything") lives in Bellingham, Washington, where he teaches high school, writes stories, and does his best to stay dry. His main project for this summer is to publish a children's picture book, a goal his mother heartily approves of.

Judith Beck ("All Aboard") lives in Berkeley, California, and works as a physician in Oakland. Her writing has appeared in numerous publications and has received such prestigious honors as the Bernice Slote Award and a Puschcart nomination, both from *Prairie Schooner*. She is presently at work on a novel.

Lori Bottoms ("Bedraggled, Bedeviled, and Beguiled") is a freelance writer who recently completed her first novel. With a nearly empty nest, she spends her spare time singing with Sweet Adelines and directing a Young Women in Harmony chorus. She resides in Broken Arrow, Oklahoma, where she is joyfully awaiting the birth of her second grandchild.

Annette M. Bower ("Mom and Gentle Bear") is a writer in a small resort town in Saskatchewan, Canada. Her writing is a midlife adventure full of challenges and joys. She is also a daughter, sister, cousin, wife, mother, god-mother, aunt, great-aunt, friend, and volunteer who used to work as a nurse.

Kathy Briccetti ("Fatherless Sons") is a freelance writer whose work has appeared in magazines and newspapers and on public radio. This piece is an excerpt from a memoir about her search for roots among three generations of absent fathers and adoptions in her family. She is also at work on a murder mystery. She lives in Berkeley, California, with her partner and two sons.

Carolyn Carasea ("Aisle of Lost Boys") lives with her husband, Jerry, and children, Caryn and Matt, in Green, Ohio. A substitute teacher, she also coedits a newsletter for parents of special needs children and lectures college students in education and medicine about understanding and working with families who have children with disabilities.

Ann Hagman Cardinal ("The Linebacker and the Sparkly Pink Pumps") is a Latina writer living in Vermont with her husband, Doug, and seven-year-old son, Carlos. She is the national marketing director for Union Institute and University and a freelance writer. Her column, Café Con Lupe, appears in local and national publications.

Bobbie Christmas ("Roses and Rodents and Mom, Oh Yeah!") lives in quiet Woodstock, Georgia, a suburb of Atlanta. She is a book editor, freelance writer, and author of *Write in Style* (Cardoza Publishing, 2004). Her son, Sandy, and daughter-in-law, Nancy, live in Vienna, Virginia. This is her second story in the *Cup of Comfort* book series.

Judi Christy ("What Goes Around") has been writing since grade school and now earns a living with this habit she refuses to break. This journalism major, multipublished author, and veteran *Cup of Comfort* contributor is also an eBay fanatic and Webmaster of artsinstark.com. She lives in Green, Ohio, with her patient husband and two creative children.

Karna J. Converse ("Speaking Son-ese") is a full-time mom and a part-time writer whose work has been published in several regional publications. She lives in Storm Lake, Iowa, with her husband and three children—all of whom provide her with many anecdotes for essays.

Darlene Craviotto ("The Pediatrician Visit"), a professional screenwriter and playwright, wrote *Love Is Never Silent* for Hallmark Hall of Fame, which won an Emmy for Outstanding Drama Special and also garnered her an Emmy nomination for the script. She lives in Santa Barbara, California, with her husband, two children, and a hyperactive beagle named Nike.

Christopher Cumo ("Sediment of the Past"), a native of Italy, makes his home in Canton, Ohio, with his wife and two daughters. A staff writer and assistant editor of *The Adjunct Advocate* magazine, he is also the author of two books and more than 400 published articles, essays, book reviews, works of fiction, and poetry.

Shari Bowes Deaven ("How I Came to Know Larry Evans") lives in Harrisburg, Pennsylvania, with her husband and daughter. She writes short stories, poetry, and magazine articles, using her writing to heal from the death of her son, Mike, and to convey the love of Christ to others.

Tracy L. Doerr ("Love Is a Tractor") is a freelance writer and editor whose work has appeared in publications across North America. She resides in Brampton, Ontario, Canada, with her son, Dylan, and her partner, Brian. When not racing cars across the kitchen floor, she is at work on her first novel.

Peggy Duffy ("The Anole Story") lives in north Virginia, where she writes and also works in real estate. Her short stories and essays have appeared in magazines, newspapers, literary journals, anthologies, and online publications.

Debbie Farmer ("The Other Woman") is an essayist, columnist, and author of *Don't Put Lipstick on the Cat!* Her award-winning syndicated column, Family Daze, reaches more than 400,000 readers, and her essays have appeared in numerous publications, including *Reader's Digest*, the

Washington Post, the *Christian Science Monitor*, and *Family Circle*. She lives in northern California.

Rosalie DiMichele Ferguson ("A Gracious Thing") is a retired English teacher who lived in Idaho for twenty-four years. Rearing three sons and teaching left only the early-morning hours for writing. In 1999, she returned to her home base of Ohio, where she currently tutors students from foreign countries and writes to her heart's content.

Judy L. Forney ("The Writing on the Wall") is a native of Washington State, where she works as a writer. She and her husband are also avid buyers/sellers of weird junk, especially toy robots. She has three boys she's very proud of, even when they stow sandwiches under their beds.

Cheryl Glowacki ("Reverse Psychology") resides in Berrien Springs, Michigan, with her supportive husband, Rick. She thanks her son, Scott Strzyzykowski, for being the star of her first published essay, her daughter Shannon for introducing her to the *Cup of Comfort* book series, and her daughters Stephanie and Sarah for encouraging her to write.

Marge D. Hansen ("Using Our Words") lives with her husband in Lafayette, Colorado. She is a freelance writer and editor and contributes regularly to national magazines and Web sites. Her first book, *An English Experience—Exploring the Backroads and Byways of Gloucestershire, Wiltshire and Hampshire*, was released in 2003.

Kira Hardison ("Rockn Da Nose") lives in Colorado. She is a homeschooling mother of three boys. When not retrieving things from their noses, she writes.

Susan Sleman Hare ("Chaos Theory of Teenage Boys"), a former marketing executive, lives in northern California with her husband, two sons, two dogs, and a fish named Henry Higgins. Her personal essays have been published in the *Christian Science Monitor* and the Knight Ridder newspapers. She is currently working on a series of lighthearted mystery novels.

Sarah L. Hess ("Heavensent") lives in Phoenix, Arizona, with her husband and nineteen-month-old son, Ethan. After graduating from Northern Arizona University, she worked in human resources at a resort until the birth of her son. She is now a stay-at-home mom and is pursuing her lifelong passion for writing.

Inez Hollander ("Hero") got tired of footnotes and quit academia to indulge in creative writing. Her essays have appeared in the *Cup of Comfort* series as well as in *Moxie*, *The Philosophical Mother*, and other publications. Her memoir, *Awakening from the American Dream* (Archipel, 2004), chronicles life after the "dot bomb."

Diana Jordan ("Outside the Box") reviews books and interviews hundreds of authors each year for Associated Press Radio's *Between the Lines* and *Portfolio*, aired on hundreds of stations around the nation, as well as for

BarnesandNoble.com's "Meet the Writers." She is also AM Northwest's book reviewer on the ABC-TV affiliate and anchors a morning news show on KLTH-FM radio in Portland, Oregon.

Deb Kalmbach ("Feet That Leave, Hearts That Stay") is an author and speaker, and coauthor of *Because I Said Forever: Embracing Hope in a Not-So-Perfect Marriage*. She and her husband, Randy, make their home in Washington's beautiful Methow Valley. Their grown sons, Chris and Jeremy "Owen," live in the Seattle area.

Penny J. Leisch ("Like a Rock") is an award-winning poet and photographer residing in Chandler, Arizona. In addition to writing instructional materials, book and film reviews, travel features, essays, articles, and a family activities column, she teaches writing and photography.

Wendy Lichtman ("Courtside") is a freelance writer who lives in Berkeley, California. She has written four books of fiction for young adults, and her personal essays have appeared in several national publications, including the *New York Times*, the *Washington Post* magazine, the *San Francisco Chronicle*, *Good Housekeeping*, and *Parenting* magazine.

Gary B. Luerding ("The Sunny Side") is a retired Army sergeant and school district employee living in O'Brien, Oregon. He has been married to his lovely wife, Lynne, for forty-one years, and they have three children and eight grandchildren. He enjoys gardening and fishing, and still plays the piano.

Barbara Marshak ("Some Distance Now Required") is a freelance writer currently dividing her time between writing and working in the First Judicial District Courts. Her true passion, however, is fiction, and she is currently pursuing publication of her first novel. She resides in the Twin Cities (Minnesota) with her husband and family.

Tricia L. McDonald ("I Linger") is a published author who lives, works, and creates in Grand Haven, Michigan. She shares her home with her husband, Mike, and children, Nicole and Jake. She is a member of Peninsula Writers.

Kathryn McKay ("Boys on the Wall"), a graduate of the University of Delaware and Johns Hopkins University, lives in Bethesda, Maryland, with her husband and two sons. She has been published in *Family Circle*, the *Washington Post*, *Baltimore Magazine*, and parenting publications nationwide. She is the author of Fodor's *Around Washington, D.C. with Kids*.

Jennifer Meyer ("Tender Is the Night") is a freelance writer living in Eugene, Oregon. Her first novel, *Missing Pieces*, is awaiting publication, and she is working on a second. She has two sons, ages twenty and sixteen. She and her wife, Kate, were recently wed after twenty-two years together.

JoEllen Murphy ("Take Me Out to the Ball Game") is a hospital social worker living in western New York. She is the mother of five and grandmother of six. She enjoys trips to Las Vegas with her husband, and she is a big fan of the West Seneca East Trojans and the New York Yankees.

Sharon Nesbit ("Brave Hearts") is a longtime reporter/columnist with *The Gresham Outlook*. She and her husband, Bill, raised their children in Troutdale, Oregon, and now watch those children raise families of their own. The little boy in her story sent his own first grader off to school last year.

Jane Ness ("Out of the Darkness") is a teacher, writer, and mother of three, who lives in Columbia, South Carolina. She is training to run in her first marathon and working on a novel set in the 1960s.

Janet L. Oakley ("Sons and Streams") is the educational curator at a county museum in Washington State. She also writes social studies curricula for schools and historical organizations as well as novels and essays. Her future husband took her fishing for the first time four months after they met.

Mary Paliescheskey ("Broken Monkey") is a freelance writer and artist. She lives in Southern California with a house full of boys: her husband and three sons. Once upon a time, she was a research scientist. Today, she homeschools her children.

Sharon Palmer ("Roller Coaster Ride of Love") is a registered dietitian, freelance writer, and mother of two boys. She and her husband have raised their family in the small town of Bradbury, nestled in the chaparral hills overlooking Los Angeles. They enjoy scouting their backyard wilderness and have spied brown bears, bobcats, rattlesnakes, fox, and coyotes prowling about.

Betty Peterson ("An Unexpected Truth") is currently a professor of English at Somerset Community College in Somerset, Kentucky. She writes in all genres and has published in *English Journal*, *Seventeen*, and *Appalachian Heritage*, to name a few, in addition to having had several plays produced. She was recently commissioned through a grant from the NEA to adapt Harriette Arnow's novel *The Dollmaker* for stage.

Linda Holland Rathkopf ("Can You Hear Me Now?") is a writer and artist. Her artwork has been shown throughout the Northeast, and three of her plays—"Who Stole the Mona Lisa?" "The Kindling Effect," and "The Airport Encounter"—have been produced in New York City. She makes her home in Brooklyn, New York.

Natalina C. Rodriguez ("Sure, I Know"), after receiving a master's degree from Florida State University, worked for the U.S. Census Bureau and then spent twenty years alongside her husband on assignment in Latin America. She now lives in Easton, Pennsylvania, where retirement has allowed her to fulfill her love of writing.

Stephen D. Rogers ("Me in the Middle") is a stay-at-home dad who lives in Buzzards Bay, Massachusetts. He can't wait to share the news of this story's being published with his mother. His daughter doesn't seem too impressed by the announcement.

Carmen Rosado ("Guess What?") lives in North Brunswick, New Jersey, where she is a stay-at-home mom of twin boys, who are her inspiration. A writer of essays and children's stories, she holds a bachelor's degree in business administration and loves to read and travel.

Terry Miller Shannon ("Naming Names") loves to have her grandkids visit her home in the Pacific Northwest. She is the coauthor, with her older son, Tim Warner, of the rhyming children's book *Tub Toys* (Tricycle Press, 2002).

Susan J. Siersma ("A Prince by Any Other Name"), a native New Jerseyan, is a freelance writer and full-time caregiver, who most enjoys spending time with family. She dedicates "A Prince" to all those taking care of loved ones with Alzheimer's disease.

Thomas Smith ("To the Bat Cave, Mama!") is an award-winning writer and playwright. He's crazy about his wife, has two (mostly) housebroken dogs, and picks a pretty fair lead guitar in his church's praise band.

Carol Tyx ("Crossing the Boundary Waters"), who continues crossing the boundary waters to mother adult children, teaches writing at Mt. Mercy College. Although she loves visits from her sons, she lives joyously (most of the time) with a very talkative cat as her companion in Iowa City, Iowa.

Jeanette Valentine ("Marching Orders"), a freelance writer in the San Francisco Bay area, has been obsessed with her craft since first grade, when she won a writing contest by penning thirty-eight stories. (The second runner-up wrote seven.) With her son, Lamont, in college 3,000 miles away, she now applies her expert nurturing skills to Mimi, a gray-and-white tabby cat.

Peggy Vincent ("Ice Cubes"), a retired midwife, is now a full-time writer with many published essays and articles to her credit, including several in the *Cup of Comfort* book series. Her memoir, *Baby Catcher: Chronicles of a Modern Midwife*, was published in 2002 (Scribner), and screen rights were recently sold. She lives in Oakland, California, with her husband; their three adult children live nearby.

Leslie Terkel Wake ("Tethered") lives with her family in Hudson, Ohio. A full-time mom and "guitar lady" at a local children's hospital, she recently immersed herself in writing and is "exhilarated by guiding thoughts into a string of words that balances details with emotions."

Rachel Wallace-Oberle ("The Beautiful Years"), a resident of Elmira, Ontario, Canada, enjoys walking, classical music, and canaries. A freelance writer with an education in both journalism and broadcasting, she has written for numerous publications, works for the Foundation for International Development, and cohosts a weekly radio program.

Amy Walton ("A Date to Remember") lives in Virginia Beach, Virginia, where she is a local TV anchor as well as a museum educator/volunteer coordinator. She also occasionally writes a story or two, when she can stay seated for more than a minute. She is the mother of two young men and a Dalmatian.

Ellen H. Ward ("Pigs in Combat Gear"), a freelance writer and editor, lives in the mountains of North Georgia with her husband, Kevin, and their three children, Megan, Rachel, and Sean. She has had numerous articles published on the subjects of family, lifestyle, medical, travel, and political issues.

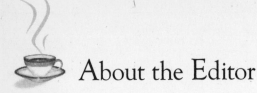

About the Editor

Colleen Sell has long believed in the power of story to inspire and enrich our lives. Storytelling is both her passion and profession, and with it, she has fed her family and her soul for more than twenty-five years.

Colleen has published hundreds of articles and essays as well as numerous books, including *10-Minute Zen* and ten volumes of the *Cup of Comfort* book series. She also has been a magazine editor-in-chief, journalist, columnist, book editor, and copywriter.

She and her husband, T. N. Trudeau, share a Victorian on a lavender farm in the Pacific Northwest, where her son is a frequent and welcome guest.

The *Cup of Comfort* Series!

All titles are $9.95 unless otherwise noted.
